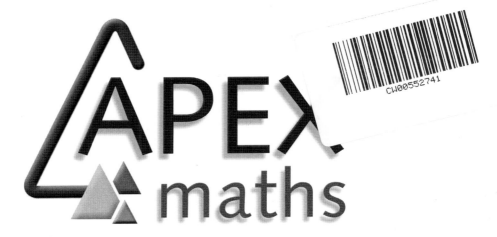

APEX maths

2

Extension *for all* through problem solving

Teacher's Handbook
Year 2 / Primary 3

Ann Montague-Smith

Paul Harrison

Rosebank Primary

CAMBRIDGE
UNIVERSITY PRESS

PUBLISHED BY THE PRESS SYNDICATE OF THE UNIVERSITY OF CAMBRIDGE
The Pitt Building, Trumpington Street, Cambridge, United Kingdom

CAMBRIDGE UNIVERSITY PRESS
The Edinburgh Building, Cambridge CB2 2RU, UK
40 West 20th Street, New York, NY 10011-4211, USA
477 Williamstown Road, Port Melbourne, VIC 3207, Australia
Ruiz de Alarcón 13, 28014 Madrid, Spain
Dock House, The Waterfront, Cape Town 8001, South Africa

http://www.cambridge.org

First published 2003

Printed in Dubai by Oriental Press

Typefaces Frutiger, Swift   *System* QuarkXPress® 4.03

A catalogue record for this book is available from the British Library

ISBN 0 521 75489 5 paperback

Authors Ann Montague-Smith, Paul Harrison

ACKNOWLEDGEMENTS
Content editing by Beverley Uttley
Cover design by Karen Thomas
Text illustration by Katy Taggart
Project management by Cambridge Publishing Management Limited
The authors and publishers would like to thank the schools and individuals who trialled lessons.

Contents

Introduction

About Apex Maths   **6**
- *Teacher's materials*   6
- *Pupils' materials*   6

Approaches to problem solving   **7**
- *Lesson timing*   7

Features of the lesson plans   **8**

Lesson structure   **10**
- *Differentiation*   10
- *Questioning techniques*   10
- *Optional adult input*   10
- *Class organisation*   11
- *Resources*   11
- *Assessment*   11

Scope and sequence chart   **12**

Scotland 5–14 Guidelines   **14**

Northern Ireland Lines of Development   **15**

Oral and mental problem solving starters   **16**

Lesson plans

1 Frame it!   **22**
This activity involves searching for number patterns, through exploring the perimeters of squares.

2 Number line   **24**
The numbers 1 to 100 include 1-, 2- and 3-digit numbers. Children are asked to find out how many of each digit are needed to make all of the numbers from 1 to 100.

3 How old is Granny?   **26**
Children use what they know about place value and odd and even numbers to find an unknown number.

4 Number generator   **28**
Children explore how many different numbers they can make using the digits 1 to 9.

5 Next-door numbers   **30**
Within their given number range, children explore numbers that can be made by totalling consecutive numbers.

6   What's the rule?   32

Children identify number sorting rules, using properties of numbers such as odd numbers, or multiples of 5.

7   Fraction flags   34

Children investigate different ways of finding a given fraction of a rectangular grid.

8   Dart totals   36

Children find different ways of making totals from numbers 1 to 20.

9   Arithmagons   38

Each arithmagon must have a given total for each side, using 3 numbers chosen from 1 to 6, and with all 6 numbers used for each problem.

10   Four in a row   40

The problem involves finding differences between pairs of numbers.

11   Square numbers   42

Using addition, children investigate whether the total of diagonally opposite numbers in squares of numbers on a 100 square will always be the same.

12   Solve it!   44

Each digit 1 to 9 must be placed on a grid so that the difference between any joined pair of numbers is odd.

13   Equal totals   46

Using just the numbers 3, 4, 5 and 6, children find ways of making each row, diagonal and column in a 4 × 4 square have the same total.

14   Make fifteen   48

Children find trios of cards that total 15.

15   Counter shapes   50

Children explore which multiplications have the same totals.

16   Two-dice totals   52

This problem involves finding number pairs that make totals to 12. Children use 2 dice and try to cover all of the numbers on the grid. As they play the game again, they will find that some different combinations of dice scores produce the same totals.

17   Animal quackers   54

Children find different ways of combining multiples of 2 and 4 to make 32.

18   Digits   56

The problem involves finding multiples of 10 and 20.

19   Pocket money   58

An investigation into finding the range of possible values for a given number of coins.

20   Leapfrog   60

Children search for numbers with common multiples.

21 Make a shape   **62**
Children listen to and use the mathematical language of shape, position and direction, and give and follow instructions carefully.

22 Shape pairs   **64**
The photocopy master contains twelve shapes to be cut out and paired to make the shape shown in the textbook.

23 Cube shapes   **66**
Children explore the different shapes that can be made with 4 cubes. The problem is similar to the well-known pentominoes investigation, but easier.

24 Four-sided shapes   **68**
Using 2 tiles at a time, children investigate which 4-sided shapes they can make.

25 Four the same   **70**
Children explore fitting together 4 of the same shape in order to cover a square.

26 Triangle trap   **72**
Children explore different shapes and sizes of triangles.

27 Favourite TV programmes   **74**
Children are asked to fill a videotape with programmes. On the textbook page there is a programme listing for a Saturday, with times to the quarter hour.

28 Ticker timer   **76**
Children make their own, non-standard timer, then try to work out for how long it will rock. They use it to measure everyday events in the classroom.

29 Sand weight challenge   **78**
This investigation involves combining weights, halving quantities to make new amounts, and an understanding of multiples of 20 and 50.

30 Hoop roll   **80**
Children estimate and measure the circumferences of circular objects.

Useful mathematical information   82

Photocopy Masters   91

Introduction

About Apex Maths

Apex Maths uses problem solving to address the needs of the more able and also provides extension and enrichment opportunities for children of all abilities. This allows Apex Maths to be used within the context of the whole-class daily mathematics lesson, because it reflects the philosophy of the National Numeracy Strategy *Framework for teaching mathematics*.

Thirty detailed lesson plans are presented in the Teacher's Handbook. Each focuses on a core problem or investigation and is differentiated in various ways so that children of all abilities can work at their level on the same basic problem.

The lessons address all of the problem solving objectives of the *Framework* and span all *Framework* strands.

The problems are richer and deeper than the relatively straightforward word problems suggested by the *Framework* examples, thereby helping children to develop thinking skills. They provide contexts in which children can apply and extend their mathematical skills and understanding, and consolidate their problem solving skills.

The teaching approach adopted throughout allows children to use enquiry, creative thinking and reasoning skills to solve a problem, with input from the teacher in the form of probing questions and occasional suggestions and hints. A carefully designed plenary encourages children to discuss their reasoning and evaluate the strategies used.

Teacher's materials

The Teacher's Handbook includes:

Scope and sequence chart
This lists all the problems together with the problem solving objectives addressed (from the *Framework for teaching mathematics*), the likely outcome levels for each ability group for Attainment Target 1 (Using and applying mathematics) in the *National Curriculum for England: Mathematics* and the *Framework* topics addressed by each problem.

Scotland 5–14 Guidelines
A chart linking each lesson to related strands in *Curriculum and Assessment in Scotland, National Guidelines: Mathematics 5–14*.

Northern Ireland Lines of Development
A table linking each lesson to related *Northern Ireland Lines of Development* (Levels 2 and 3).

Oral and mental problem solving starters
A bank of oral and mental starters with a problem solving slant, which can be used at the start of any lesson.

Lesson plans
These are presented in double-page spreads. A blueprint on pages 8–9 explains the features of the plans.

The lesson plans feature different types of problems, including:

- investigations requiring the identification of patterns and the making of generalisations;
- number puzzles and investigations that require reasoning about numbers;
- complex 'real-life', multi-stage problems involving a range of mathematical techniques;
- calculation problems, in which combinations of known values are used to find unknown values.

Useful mathematical information
This is a bank of additional mathematical information. It might explain a particular concept or look at a particular problem in greater depth.

Pupils' materials

Problems are presented for children in the Pupil's Textbook and/or using Photocopy Masters (PCMs) from the Teacher's Handbook.

Where parts of the page are numbered in the Textbook, this generally indicates a progression in the complexity of the problem. The Differentiation section of the Lesson plan indicates which parts of the pupils' material are intended for which ability group.

Sometimes, differentiation of a problem involves giving clues or additional direction to the Average or Less able groups.

Within the Textbook, a red tinted box indicates text that is relevant to all the problem levels and that all children should read. Text for children to copy is tinted light blue. Equipment needed by children is shown in red text.

The Textbook also contains a glossary of mathematical and problem solving terms used in the problems.

Approaches to problem solving

When working at solving problems, children benefit from discussing what they have to do and how they might go about this. This can be as part of a whole-class discussion, or in pairs or small groups. On occasions, the discussion may not seem to be contributing to the resolution of the problem, but it can be allowed to continue for a short while so that children gain confidence in putting forward their ideas and using mathematical vocabulary appropriately.

Problem solving offers excellent opportunities to develop thinking and reasoning skills. This should be encouraged so that children become confident in using these skills not just when involved in problem solving, but in all their mathematical work and in other curriculum areas. Children should be encouraged to:

- choose the appropriate mathematics for the problem and explain why they made their choice;
- be confident enough to try different strategies, evaluate their effectiveness and recognise when their chosen strategy is not effective;
- draw a picture or diagram or use equipment to aid understanding;
- try a simpler case in order to understand how the problem could be solved;

- work in a systematic way, recording work in a logical order, so that it is clear to others what has been tried;
- look for a pattern;
- form hypotheses, asking and answering questions such as *What if . . . ?*;
- consider if there are other, and better, solutions;
- try extensions to the problem, asking and answering *What could I try next?*;
- report what they have done in order to solve the problem, speaking clearly and using appropriate mathematical vocabulary.

Because children approach problems from different perspectives, including different experiences of mathematics and varying degrees of understanding, it is important to accept a range of strategies for solving a problem and a variety of solutions. By creating a comfortable atmosphere in which it is safe to put forward a view, idea or solution, children's confidence in their problem solving abilities will increase. It is also important to follow a problem through to a satisfactory solution, so that children can learn from others and improve their understanding of what is expected from them and ways of going about finding solutions. Expect your successes to improve as children's experience and confidence increases.

Sometimes when you ask a question, children will not respond immediately. Make use of silence; give children time to think through what has been asked so that they can formulate a response.

Lesson timing

The problem solving lessons in Apex Maths are designed to last for the length of a normal daily maths lesson. However, children's response to a given problem may determine whether the lesson could be extended for some minutes or returned to in another maths lesson.

Features of the lesson plans

Resources

Any Textbook pages, PCMs and equipment needed by the teacher, plus resources that children might choose to use, depending upon the problem solving approach they decide to take.

Key vocabulary

The main problem solving and mathematical terms associated with the problem.

What's the problem?

A brief description of the problem and the mathematics that might be encountered, bearing in mind that children may use different areas of mathematics to solve the problem in their own way.

Problem solving objectives

The key problem solving objectives for the lesson.

Differentiation

Suggested activities for different ability groups. Children should not feel restricted to one activity and should, where appropriate, be allowed to move on to a more demanding activity.

Introducing the problem

Ideas for introducing the problem to children before they consider their strategy and begin the investigation.

Minimum prior experience

The minimum mathematical experience required for children to participate in the lesson. This will help you to decide when in the year to use each lesson.

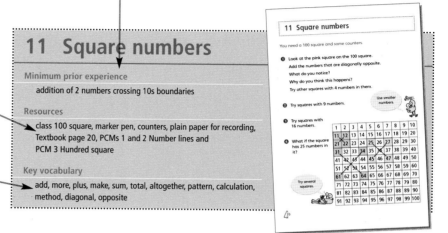

---

11 Square numbers

Minimum prior experience

addition of 2 numbers crossing 10s boundaries

Resources

class 100 square, marker pen, counters, plain paper for recording, Textbook page 20, PCMs 1 and 2 Number lines and PCM 3 Hundred square

Key vocabulary

add, more, plus, make, sum, total, altogether, pattern, calculation, method, diagonal, opposite

What's the problem?

Using addition, children investigate whether the total of diagonally opposite numbers in squares of numbers on a 100 square will always be the same.

Problem solving objectives

- Investigate a general statement about familiar numbers or shapes by finding examples that satisfy it.
- Solve mathematical problems or puzzles, recognise simple patterns and relationships, generalise and predict. Suggest extensions by asking 'What if . . . ?' or 'What could I try next?'

Differentiation

More able: Textbook page 20, problems 1 to 4. Investigate squares with 4, 9 and 16 numbers.

Average: Textbook page 20, problems 1 to 3. Investigate squares with 4 and 9 numbers.

Less able: Textbook page 20, problems 1 and 2. Investigate squares with 4 numbers.

Introducing the problem

Say the problem: *Look at the 100 square in your textbook. Look at the small pink square with opposite numbers of 11 and 22, then 12 and 21. What happens if you total each of these pairs of diagonally opposite numbers?* (The total is 33 each time.) Discuss quickly what is meant by 'diagonally opposite'. *What if you choose a different square? What do you notice? Use your 100 square to try out different squares.*

42

Children can use PCM 3 and write on it if they find that helpful. Ask them to think about how they will record their results.

Teacher focus for activity

All abilities: If any children have difficulty with the addition involved, suggest that they use number lines to help them, as well as pencil-and-paper jottings. Encourage children to record their work carefully. They can draw arrows in their squares to remind them which numbers to total.

More able: Encourage children to work with larger numbers on the square and to move on quickly from a 4 square to a 9 square and then to a 16 square.

Average: Children may have more success if they make their squares using the numbers from 1 to 30, at least to begin with.

Less able: Children may be more comfortable working with smaller numbers from 1 to 20, making just a 4-number square.

As children work, ask questions, such as:
- *How did you work that out?*
- *If you chose that small square of numbers, would the opposite numbers total the same? Why is that, do you think?*
- *What if you chose a larger square? What do you think would happen then?*
- *How did you total those numbers? What strategies did you use?*

Teacher focus for activity

Suggestions for facilitating the problem solving process and for developing children's problem solving skills as they work. It includes suggestions for probing questions, discussion points and areas to look out for.

Optional adult input

Provides a focus for assisting with particular groups if additional adult help is available.

Optional adult input

Work with the Less able group. Children can all work to total the diagonal numbers in an agreed square. Encourage children to think about how they can record what they find out.

Plenary

1 Use a large, class 100 square. Invite individual children to draw around one of their 2 × 2 squares, draw in the arrows and give the totals, which should be the same. Repeat this for 3 × 3 squares, then for 4 × 4 squares.

Ask:

- *What do you notice about the totals each time?* (They are the same for each square.)
- *Why do you think that is?*

Invite children to speculate about this and praise them for their thoughts. Some may have noticed that if each pair of numbers is compared, there are always the same tens and units, but formed into different numbers. For example for the number pairs 15 and 37 and 17 and 35, each pair has a 10, a 30, a 7 and a 5, so that the same tens and units are being totalled.

2 Ask:

- *Suppose we chose a 5 × 5 square. What do you think would happen then?*

Draw around the following square:

3	4	5	6	7
13	14	15	16	17
23	24	25	26	27
33	34	35	36	37
43	44	45	46	47

Ask children to total the diagonally opposite numbers in their heads: 3 + 47 = 50 and 7 + 43 = 50

Invite a child to choose another 5 × 5 square, then a 6 × 6 one, and check again that the opposite diagonal numbers always total the same. Finally, total the opposite corners of the 100 square – that is, 1 and 100 and 10 and 91.

Ask for examples of how children recorded their results. Discuss how, where the addition sums have been written down, it is possible to see the relationship between the 2 pairs of numbers in each case.

Development

What could we try next with this problem? Suggestions could include trying 6 × 6, 7 × 7 . . . squares or trying diagonal opposites in rectangles. These ideas could form the basis for further investigation or for homework.

See **Useful mathematical information**, pages 84–85, for further information about the addition of diagonal numbers in a 100 square.

Solutions

The addition of opposite numbers in a square gives the same total. For example:

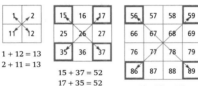

1 + 12 = 13
2 + 11 = 13

15 + 37 = 52
17 + 35 = 52

56 + 89 = 145
59 + 86 = 145

Plenary

The main whole-class interactive teaching part of the lesson, with suggestions for discussion of solutions to the problem, the methods used, problem solving skills and the maths involved.

Development

Ideas for children to develop the problem, perhaps at home. They can also be used for children who manage to complete a problem early on in the lesson. This section is not always included.

Useful mathematical information reference

A reference to indicate where you can find additional information about the mathematics involved in a problem

Solutions

Solutions to the problem at all levels for quick reference.

Lesson structure

Lessons have the recommended 3-part structure, but there is a slightly different emphasis on each part. It is intended that children will solve the problem in their own way, so your input at the start of the activity is comparatively brief and is mainly concerned with introducing the problem and checking that children understand what is required.

The main teaching will take place indirectly – through probing questions, hints and suggestions as children work. Direct teaching takes place in the plenary, when solutions, problem solving methods and the mathematics involved are discussed. The plenary therefore contains much greater detail than the problem introduction. It offers opportunities for children to:

- use appropriate vocabulary;
- compare their strategies and solutions;
- listen to explanations and develop their understanding of mathematical ideas and strategies;
- ask and answer questions.

Differentiation

The problems in this book are differentiated in various ways:

- By level of difficulty

  Here there are different activities for different ability groups. Early finishers may be able to progress to an activity for a higher ability group.

- By outcome

  Here children are expected to approach the problem in more or less sophisticated ways, applying mathematical knowledge and understanding at their own level.

- By resource used as support

  Here children can choose different resources to support them, such as working mentally, using pencil and paper, using an empty number line or using a 100 square. Sometimes a hint may be provided for lower ability groups.

- By level of support

  Here, especially where additional adults are available, groups can be targeted for specific support.

Questioning techniques

There will be many opportunities to ask questions during a problem solving lesson.

Closed questions will give a response of yes or no, or will elicit specific knowledge. They can be used to check understanding. Examples include:

- *Do you understand?* (yes/no)
- *What is half of 100?* (50)

Open questions allow children the opportunity to give a range of responses. Examples include:

- *Which two numbers added together would give the answer 20?* (15 + 5; 12 + 8; 10 + 10; 19 + 1 . . .)
- *How could you solve this problem?*

Probing questions are nearly always open in the sense that they require a carefully thought out answer, through which children explain their mathematics. These questions will give you the opportunity to assess their understanding. Examples include:

- *How did you work that out? Is there another way?*
- *What would happen if the numbers were changed to . . . ? Would that make a difference? Why is that?*
- *Roughly what answer do you expect to get? How did you come to that estimate?*

Optional adult input

Children may need support and encouragement while they gain familiarity and confidence with working in a new way, or if they have limited experience of solving problems. You may find it helpful, if possible, to arrange for some additional classroom help, particularly when first using this resource.

There are suggestions in each lesson plan as to which group any additional adult could help with and in what way. Here are some general suggestions about how to make best use of an additional adult:

- Fully brief them about the problem for that lesson and what your expectations are for each ability group.
- Make sure that they understand that children should be allowed to solve a problem in their own way, even if, at times, it seems that they are going down a blind alley.
- Encourage use of suggested probing questions from the **Teacher focus for activity** section of each lesson. Also suggest the following 'catch all' questions:
  - *Can you explain what you have done so far?*
  - *Why did you do that?*
  - *What are you going to do next?*

Class organisation

The lessons in Apex Maths have been specifically designed as whole-class numeracy lessons.

The differentiated ways in which the problems are presented make them ideal for mixed-age classes. They are also highly suitable for schools in which children are set according to ability for mathematics lessons. The higher ability sets can work on the main problem, while the average and lower ability sets work on the differentiated presentations of the problem.

In mixed ability classes, children should be broadly grouped in the classroom according to ability. This will facilitate group discussion with the teacher if needed. It will also avoid children 'borrowing' clues or additional directions provided for children of a lesser ability.

Children should ideally work in pairs or threes when they are working on a problem or investigation. This will stimulate discussion – an essential component of the problem solving process.

Resources

Simple resources, all of which are readily available, will be needed to support these activities. Some may be essential to the successful outcome of the activity. Others should be made available so that children can make decisions on resources needed.

General resources that may be useful include:
- individual whiteboards
- number lines (PCMs 1 and 2)
- hundred square (PCM 3)
- digit cards (PCM 4)
- 0–100 number cards
- counters and centimetre cubes
- interlocking cubes
- squared and dotty paper (centimetre squares)
- pin boards (geoboards) and elastic bands.

Assessment

While children are working at the problem and during the plenary, target pairs and individuals in order to assess their skills in problem solving. Use probing questions, such as the examples given under **Questioning techniques** (page 10) and those given within the teacher's notes for the lesson. By targeting specific children during each problem solving lesson it is possible to ensure that all children will be assessed through discussion over time.

Look for signs of consistency in approach to a given problem. Make sure that children read all of the data and are able to decide which data is relevant and which should be discarded.

When discussing children's work, take the opportunity to identify whether they have understood the mathematics involved. This is an ideal time to check whether there are any misconceptions that need remedying.

Watch for children who rely too heavily on their partner for:
- **how to solve the problem**: Does the child understand what the problem involves?
- **mathematical calculations**: Does the child understand which calculation strategies and procedures to use, and can they use them themselves?
- **recording the problem**: Is the child able to suggest how the results might be presented?
- **answering open and probing questions and reporting back in the plenary**: Is the child able to articulate their thinking? Does the child have the appropriate vocabulary and can they use it appropriately to express mathematical ideas and explanations? Are they given enough response time?

During the problem solving lesson, take time to stand back and observe what the children are doing.
- Do children cooperate?
- Are they working collaboratively?
- Do they both contribute to the discussion or does one dominate and take the lead?
- Do they use appropriate mathematical language in order to express their ideas?

Scope and sequence chart

This chart lists all the problems together with:

- the problem solving objectives addressed (from the *NNS Framework for teaching mathematics*);
- the possible outcome levels for each ability group for Attainment Target 1 (Using and applying mathematics) in the *National Curriculum for England: Mathematics*;
- the *Framework* topics addressed by each problem.

Because children will solve problems in different ways, using different aspect of mathematics, the specific *Framework* objectives that will be addressed will vary. For this reason, only the topics that are likely to be addressed have been referenced.

* Indicates that the general mathematical content may extend the Most able beyond the Year 2 objectives in the *Framework for teaching mathematics*.

Problem	Choose and use appropriate operations and efficient calculation strategies . . .	Solve mathematical problems or puzzles . . . Suggest extensions by asking 'What if . . .?' or 'What could I try next?'	Investigate a general statement about familiar numbers or shapes by finding examples that satisfy it.	Explain how a problem was solved orally and, where appropriate, in writing.	Use mental addition . . . to solve simple word problems . . . using 1 or 2 steps. Explain how the problem was solved.	Recognise all coins and begin to use £.p notation . . . Find totals, give change and work out which coins to pay.	Ma1 Using and applying mathematics Level/outcome (More able)	(Average)	(Less able)	Mathematical topics
1 Frame it!		■		■			Level 3	Level 2	Level 1/2	Counting, Number sequences
2 Number line		■		■			Level 3	Level 2	Level 2	Counting, Properties of number
3 How old is Granny?			■	■			Level 3	Level 2	Level 1/2	Properties of number, Place value
4 Number generator*		■		■			Level 3	Level 2	Level 1/2	Place value
5 Next-door numbers*	■	■		■			Level 3	Level 2	Level 1/2	Addition
6 What's the rule?*			■	■			Level 3	Level 2	Level 1/2	Counting, Properties of number, Number sequences
7 Fraction flags*	■	■		■			Level 3	Level 2	Level 1/2	Fractions
8 Dart totals*	■	■		■			Level 3	Level 2	Level 1/2	Addition
9 Arithmagons	■	■		■			Level 3	Level 2	Level 1/2	Addition
10 Four in a row*	■			■			Level 3	Level 2	Level 1/2	Subtraction: difference
11 Square numbers*		■		■			Level 3	Level 2	Level 1/2	Addition, Place value

Problem	Problem solving objectives involved						MA1 Using and applying mathematics Level/outcome			Mathematical topics
							More able	Average	Less able	
12 Solve it!	■	■		■			Level 3	Level 2	Level 1/2	Subtraction: difference, Properties of numbers
13 Equal totals	■	■		■			Level 3	Level 2	Level 1/2	Addition
14 Make fifteen	■	■		■			Level 3	Level 2	Level 1/2	Addition
15 Counter shapes*	■	■		■			Level 3	Level 2	Level 2	Multiplication
16 Two-dice totals	■	■		■			Level 3	Level 2	Level 1/2	Addition
17 Animal quackers*	■	■		■			Level 3	Level 2	Level 1/2	Addition, Multiplication, Number sequences
18 Digits*	■	■		■			Level 3	Level 2	Level 1/2	Multiplication, Number sequences
19 Pocket money*	■	■		■	■	■	Level 3	Level 2	Level 2	Addition, Money
20 Leapfrog*		■		■			Level 3	Level 2	Level 1/2	Multiplication, number sequences
21 Make a shape		■		■			Level 3	Level 2	Level 1/2	Properties of 2D shapes
22 Shape pairs		■		■			Level 3	Level 2	Level 1/2	Properties of 2D shapes
23 Cube shapes		■		■			Level 3	Level 2	Level 1/2	Properties of flat shapes
24 Four-sided shapes*		■		■			Level 3	Level 2	Level 1/2	Properties of 2D shapes
25 Four the same		■		■			Level 3	Level 2	Level 1/2	Properties of flat shapes
26 Triangle trap*		■		■			Level 3	Level 2	Level 1/2	Properties of triangles
27 Favourite TV programmes*	■			■	■		Level 3	Level 2	Level 2	Time, Addition
28 Ticker timer		■		■			Level 3	Level 2	Level 1/2	Time
29 Sand weight challenge*	■	■		■	■		Level 3	Level 2	Level 1/2	Weight, Addition and Subtraction
30 Hoop roll*		■		■	■		Level 3	Level 2	Level 1/2	Length

	Problem solving and enquiry	Information handling	Range and type of numbers	Money	Add and subtract	Multiply and divide	Fractions, percentages and ratio	Patterns and sequences	Functions and equations	Measure and estimate	Time	Shape, position and movement
1 Frame it!	●		●					●				
2 Number line	●	●	●					●				
3 How old is Granny?	●		●		●							
4 Number generator	●		●					●				
5 Next-door numbers	●				●			●				
6 What's the rule?	●		●					●				
7 Fraction flags	●		●				●					
8 Dart totals	●				●			●				
9 Arithmagons	●				●			●	●			
10 Four in a row	●				●				●			
11 Square numbers	●				●			●				
12 Solve it!	●				●			●				
13 Equal totals	●				●			●				
14 Make fifteen	●				●							
15 Counter shapes	●					●		●				
16 Two-dice totals	●				●			●				
17 Animal quackers	●					●		●				
18 Digits	●					●		●				
19 Pocket money	●			●	●			●				
20 Leapfrog	●							●				
21 Make a shape	●											●
22 Shape pairs	●											●
23 Cube shapes	●											●
24 Four-sided shapes	●											●
25 Four the same	●											●
26 Triangle trap	●							●				●
27 Favourite TV programmes	●				●						●	
28 Ticker timer	●									●	●	
29 Sand weight challenge	●				●					●		
30 Hoop roll	●									●		

In each activity, children will need to employ the three problem-solving steps of (1) starting, (2) doing and (3) reporting on a task. Encourage children to choose appropriate strategies at each stage, and to evaluate their choices.

Northern Ireland Lines of Development (Levels 2 and 3)

'Processes in mathematics' applies to all lessons.

Lesson		Related Lines of Development
1	Frame it!	N2.27, R3.3
2	Number line	HD3.2, N2.9, N2.11, R3.3
3	How old is Granny?	N2.9, R2.2, R2.5
4	Number generator	N2.9, N2.11, N3.2
5	Next-door numbers	N2.4, N3.4, R2.2, R2.5
6	What's the rule?	N2.9, R2.2, R2.5, R2.4, R3.3
7	Fraction flags	N2.30, N3.16
8	Dart totals	N2.1, N2.4, N2.6, N2.22, N3.4
9	Arithmagons	R2.2, R2.5
10	Four in a row	N2.5, N2.24, N2.29, N3.3, R2.2, R2.5
11	Square numbers	N2.9, N2.11, N2.22, R3.3
12	Solve it!	N2.5, N2.24, N2.29, N3.3, R2.2, R2.5
13	Equal totals	N2.1, N2.4, N3.4
14	Make fifteen	N2.4, N3.4
15	Counter shapes	N2.27, N3.10
16	Two-dice totals	N2.4
17	Animal quackers	N2.9, N3.10, R2.4
18	Digits	N2.9, R2.4, R3.3
19	Pocket money	N2.28, N3.6, N3.8, N3.15
20	Leapfrog	R2.4, R3.3
21	Make a shape	S2.3, S3.2, S3.6, S3.7
22	Shape pairs	S3.2, S3.4
23	Cube shapes	S3.3, S3.9
24	Four-sided shapes	S2.3, S3.2, S3.7, S3.10
25	Four the same	S3.3, S3.9
26	Triangle trap	S3.2, S3.10, SP3.1, SP3.2, SP3.3
27	Favourite TV programmes	T2.4, T3.1, T3.2, T4.1
28	Ticker timer	T2.1, T3.5, M2.6
29	Sand weight challenge	M2.1, M2.6, M3.5
30	Hoop roll	M3.6

Oral and mental problem solving starters

Oral and mental activities for the start of each lesson can be selected from this bank of problem solving starters or from other sources.

Resources needed for these activities include individual whiteboards and pens, digit cards and number fans.

1 Twos and fours

(properties of numbers and number sequences)

Ask children to count with you in 2s, starting from zero. Now explain that instead of saying every multiple of 2, you would like them to count every other one in their heads and to nod their heads gently at the same time, like this:

● zero, nod, four, nod, eight, nod, twelve . . .

When they are confident with this, suggest that they say the counting pattern for 4s, starting from zero, then 1, 2, 3 . . .

2 Show me number properties

(properties of numbers, rapid recall of number facts)

Children will need a pen and a small whiteboard or scrap paper on which to write. Explain: *I will say a property of a number and you write down a number that fits. When I say 'Show me', hold your boards up to show me your number.* Use examples, such as:

● an even/odd number
● a number in the 2/5/3/4/10 times table
● a number greater/less than . . .

3 Show me a number that fits

(properties of numbers)

Children will need a pen and a small whiteboard or scrap paper. Explain: *I will give you a statement about numbers and I'd like you to write a number or number sentence that fits the statement. When I say 'Show me', hold up your board for me to see.* Use examples such as:

● If a number ends in zero, then it can be divided exactly by 10 (e.g. $30 \div 10 = 3$).
● If a number ends in 2, then it is even (e.g. 22).

● Any odd number is one more than an even number (e.g. $5 = 4 + 1$).
● A multiple of 5 is half a multiple of 10 (e.g. 15 is half of 30).

4 Make a number that fits

(properties of numbers, rapid recall of number facts)

Provide a 2-spike abacus for Less able and Average children and a 3-spike abacus for More able children (see PCM 5) and 15 to 20 counters each. Explain: *I will give you an instruction and, using your counters, I would like you to make a number on the abacus that fits the statement.* Say, for example:

● *Make a number that is greater than 20 / less than 100.*
● *Make a number that has a 5 in the tens place / a 4 in the units place.*
● *Make a number that is between 16 and 30 / 116 and 130.*

5 Make a number sentence that fits

(rapid recall of number facts)

Explain that you will give a number that is the answer to a question. Ask children to think of a number sentence that has your number as its answer. Encourage children to use multiplication and division, where they can, as well as addition and subtraction. If smaller numbers are used, the whole class can respond to these. Invite various children to write their number sentences on the board. Use examples such as:

● *Think of a number sentence with the answer 1, 2, 3, 4, 5, 6, 7, 8, 9, 10 . . .*
● *How did you work that out?*
● *Are there any other number sentences we could write?*
● *What about addition/subtraction/multiplication/ division?*
● *Who could give a fraction sentence?*

6 What's my number?

(properties of numbers, rapid recall of number facts)

Explain that you are thinking of a number and that children can take turns to ask you questions so that they can work out what the number is. Tell them that you will say only *yes* or *no* in reply. For example, for 56:

- Is the number more than 50? *Yes*
- Is it more than 70? *No*
- Is it even? *Yes . . .*

When a child has guessed correctly, they can think of a number and answer yes or no to the questions.

7 Fraction challenge

(fractions)

Provide each child with 12 counters or cubes. Explain: *I will ask some fraction questions. Use your counters to help you work out the answers.* Use, for example:

- *How many is half of 12?*
- *How many is a quarter of 12?*
- *What is half / a quarter of 8?*

For the More able group:

- *What is three-quarters of 8? How did you work that out?*
- *What is a tenth of 10? A fifth? How do you know?*
- *What is a third of 12? Two thirds?*

Repeat for different quantities of counters, such as 16, 18, 20 . . ., choosing numbers with appropriate multiples.

8 Three-number totals

(understanding addition)

Explain that you will say a number and that you would like children to write down an addition sentence where they have added three numbers to make that number. For example, if you say 12, a child may write 5 + 3 + 4 = 12. For each total, check that children have a range of responses and write these on the board – seeing responses may trigger other ideas. Keep the totals between 12 and 30. If necessary, provide number lines as an aid for the Less able group. Ask:

- *How did you work that out?*
- *Does it matter in which order you add these up? Why not?*
- *Who had another idea?*

9 What comes next?

(properties of numbers, number sequences)

Begin by writing on the flipchart three numbers that form part of a number sequence, such as 30, 33 and 36. Ask *What comes next?* Ask children to explain how they worked this out, and then repeat for other sequences of numbers, including sequences that count down.

10 Differences

(understanding addition and subtraction, mental calculation strategies)

Say to children *I shall say the difference between 2 numbers. Think of a pair of numbers with that difference.* Invite various children to give pairs with that difference, and then you write the answers on the board. Seeing a range of answers will trigger others. Keep the difference a small number, so that all can respond. Encourage the More able group to respond using a wider range of number facts. Ask questions about the answers such as:

- *How did you work that out?*
- *Can you think of another pair?*

11 Make a total

(place value, mental calculation strategies)

Write some numbers on the board, such as: 8, 10, 13, 15, 19. Ask questions such as:

- *Tell me 2 numbers that would give an even total. How do you know that?*
- *Tell me 2 that would give an odd total.*
- *Give me 2 numbers whose total has an 8 in the units place.*
- *Tell me 2 numbers whose total has a 1 in the tens place.*
- *How did you work that out?*

This can be repeated with other starting numbers.

12 Odd numbers

(properties of numbers)

Say to children *Odd numbers have 1 left over when you divide by 2, but even numbers do not. Can you think of some examples to show this?*

Invite individuals to write their number sentences onto the flipchart and explain why their result is appropriate.

13 Even numbers

(properties of numbers)

Say to children *Any even number can be made by adding 2 odd numbers. Can you think of some examples to show this?*

Invite individuals to write their number sentences onto the flipchart. Ask children: *Why does this work?*

Can you explain this? (Both numbers will have remainder 1 when divided by 2, so that these two 1s can combine to make another 2, thus giving an even answer.)

14 Make number sentences

(rapid recall of number facts)

Explain to children that the answer to the question is always 15. Ask them to write 2 different number sentences on their whiteboard with the answer of 15 and, when you say '*Show me*' to hold up their whiteboard.

Write some of the sentences on the board. Challenge children to think of more number sentences that are different from those on the board.

Repeat for different totals.

15 Multiplication scores

(rapid recall of multiplication facts)

Explain that you will say a multiplication answer and that you would like children to think of a fact that this could belong to. For example, for 6, they might say 2×3, 3×2, 1×6 and 6×1. Choose answers that lie within the multiplication tables that they know. Invite children to explain how they worked out their answers. This is more fun when answers with a number of associated multiplication facts, such as 12 or 20, are chosen.

16 Dice totals

(rapid recall of addition facts, mental calculation strategies)

Explain to children that you will roll 2 dice each time, but that you will not let them see the dice. Instead, you will give them some facts and ask them to work out what the 2 dice scores might be. For example:

- *The total score is 11. What could my 2 dice scores be?* (5, 6; 6, 5)
- *One dice score is twice the other.* (1, 2; 2, 4; 3, 6)
- *Both dice have the same score. What could the score be, and what would the total be?* (1, 2; 2, 4; 3, 6; 4, 8; 5, 10; 6, 12)

17 This is my number

(properties of numbers)

Ask each child in the class to write a favourite 2-digit number on their whiteboard. Explain that you will

make a statement about numbers. If their number fits, they hold their whiteboard up. Use examples such as:

- is even/odd
- less/greater than . . .
- has an odd/even number for the tens digit
- is a multiple of . . .

Ask questions about their responses, such as:

- *How did you work that out?*
- *Can you think of another number that would fit?*

18 Fizz buzz for multiples of 2, 5 and 10

(properties of numbers and number sequences)

Explain that you would like children to count around the class, starting from zero. Every time the number is a multiple of 2, they say 'fizz', and if it is a multiple of 5, they say 'buzz'. Of course, if the number is a multiple of 2 and 5, that is a multiple of 10, they say 'fizz buzz'.

Stop every so often to ask a child to explain why they said, 'fizz', 'buzz' or 'fizz buzz'.

19 Money in my pocket

(problems involving 'real life', money or measures)

You will need some coins for this activity. Say to children: *In my pocket I have some coins. You may ask me some questions and I will answer yes or no. Try to find out how much I have and which coins there are.*

Begin with 75p, made up from 50p, 20p and 5p coins. Children may ask questions such as:

- Are all the coins silver? *Yes*
- Is there a 50 pence piece? *Yes*
- Is the total more than a pound? *No . . .*

When someone has guessed correctly, show the coins to everyone. Decide whether to put a limit on how many questions, such as 10. The child who guesses correctly could set a similar problem for the rest of the class.

20 Fizz buzz for 2s, 3s and 6s

(properties of numbers and number sequences)

Play Fizz buzz again, as in Activity 18, but this time children say 'fizz' for multiples of 2, 'buzz' for multiples of 3 and 'fizz buzz' for multiples of 6.

21 Shape thoughts

(shape and space)

Explain that you will describe some shapes and that you would like children to imagine what you say in their heads. Ask children to shut their eyes and then say: *Imagine a square. Imagine a line going through the square from the top right-hand corner to the bottom left-hand corner. What two shapes has the line made?* (triangles)

Repeat this for other shapes.

22 Symmetrical shapes

(shape and space)

Provide each table with some shape tiles, including squares, rectangles, right-angled triangles, other triangles, pentagons, hexagons and circles, and some mirrors. Say: *I will describe a shape. Decide which shape I am describing, then decide if it is symmetrical. You can use a mirror to do this if you wish.* Suggest that children work in pairs to do this. For example:

- *My shape has 3 sides and 1 right angle. Is it symmetrical?*
- *My shape has 4 right angles and its opposite sides are the same length. Is it symmetrical?*
- *My shape has no straight edges. Is it symmetrical?*

After each shape has been chosen, invite children to demonstrate whether or not the shape is symmetrical. Some shapes will have more than 1 line of symmetry.

23 Make a shape

(shape and space)

Provide each child with 5 interlocking cubes. Make a shape with 3 cubes to begin with, such as:

Describe what you have made. For example:

- *Two of my cubes are joined together.*
- *These 2 cubes are one on top of the other.*
- *My third cube is attached to the bottom cube so that I have made an L shape.*

Invite children to hold up what they have made and compare their shape with yours. Repeat this for 4-cube shapes and then 5-cube shapes.

24 Shape sort

(shape and space)

For each table, provide some shape tiles, including squares, rectangles, right-angled triangles, other triangles, pentagons, hexagons and circles. Explain to children that you will think of a shape and that you will say some of the properties of the shape. Ask children to sort the shape tiles after each property, getting rid of those that do not fit. Each pair of children should work together for this activity. Expect pairs to discuss what they are doing but to keep a sharp pace as well. For a square, you might say:

- *My shape has no curves.*
- *All the angles are the same size.*
- *My shape has 4 corners.*
- *Each side is the same length as the others.*

Repeat for other shapes.

25 Make a pattern

(shape and space)

Provide children with some shape tiles. In front of you, make a design with 2 matching tiles, such as:

Describe what you have made and ask the children to copy it. For example:

- *I have 2 square tiles.*
- *One is above the other.*
- *They are touching along one side.*

Put your shape design on the overhead projector and switch the lamp on so that children can compare their design with yours. Repeat this for other combinations of tiles; invite a child to place the tiles on the overhead projector for everyone to see, and check if they agree.

26 Pin board shapes

(shape and space)

Provide each child with a pin board and some elastic bands. Explain that you will describe a shape and that you would like children to make as many shapes that fit that description on their board as they can. This will allow children the opportunity to make the same shape, such as a square, in different sizes. Say, for example:

- *Make shapes that have 3 sides and a right angle.*
- *Make shapes that have no right angles and 3 sides.*

Give children about a minute to complete each task, and then ask them to hold up their pin board for others to compare with their own. Repeat for other shapes.

27 Time word problems

(measures – time)

You will need a teaching clock face. Provide clock faces made from PCM 17. Explain to children that you will say a time word problem and that you would like them to work out the answer. After each problem, invite a child to explain their answer, using the teaching clock face where appropriate. For example:

- *Tom gets up at 7:30 in the morning. He goes to bed at a quarter to 9 at night. How long has he been up? (13 hours 15 minutes)*
- *Janine finishes eating her lunch at a quarter past 12, then plays outside for 30 minutes before the bell rings for afternoon school. What time does the bell ring? (quarter to 1)*
- *Neena looks at her grandmother's clock. It reads half past 12. Then she looks at the video clock, which is a digital one and tells the same time. What does it read? (12:30)*

28 Time estimates

(measures – time)

Explain to children that you would like them to watch the second hand on a large clock for 10 seconds. Now explain: *Shut your eyes. When I say go, be ready to put your hand up as soon as you think 10 seconds have passed.* Ask:

- *How did you count the time?*
- *Who used a different method?*

Repeat this for different amounts of seconds, keeping the amount to no more than 30 seconds. Where children are very inaccurate in their estimates, repeat watching the second hand on the clock again.

29 Measures word problems

(measures)

Explain to children that you will ask some word problems. Ask them to put up their hands when they have an answer, and invite children to explain how they worked out the problem. Problems could include:

- *I have 50 kilograms of potatoes. How many 10 kilogram sacks can I fill with potatoes? (5)*
- *There are 40 centimetres of sticky tape on a roll. I need 5 centimetre pieces of tape for sealing some parcels. How many 5 centimetre pieces of tape can I cut from the roll? (8)*
- *A bucket holds 4 litres of water. How much water will 3 buckets hold? (12 litres)*

30 Length estimates

(measures)

Children will need some ready-cut paper strips on their tables. Measurements could include approximately: 50 cm, 10 cm, 2 cm, 4 cm, 25 cm . . . Explain that you will say a measurement and will then ask children to choose a piece of paper that they think is about the length that you say. Ask questions such as:

- *How did you decide?*
- *Why did you choose that piece of paper?*

Lesson plans

1 Frame it!

Minimum prior experience

counting in 4s

Resources

interlocking cubes, squared paper, plain paper,
Textbook pages 4 and 5

Key vocabulary

pattern, how many . . . ?, count, multiple of, predict, rule,
relationship

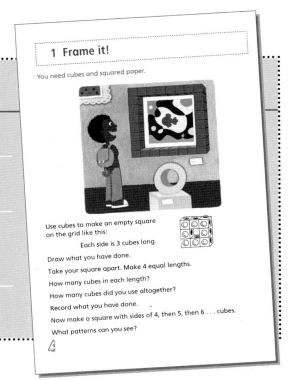

1 Frame it!

You need cubes and squared paper.

Use cubes to make an empty square
on the grid like this:

Each side is 3 cubes long.

Draw what you have done.

Take your square apart. Make 4 equal lengths.

How many cubes in each length?

How many cubes did you use altogether?

Record what you have done.

Now make a square with sides of 4, then 5, then 6 . . . cubes.

What patterns can you see?

What's the problem?

This activity involves searching for number patterns
by exploring the perimeters of squares.

Problem solving objectives

- Solve mathematical problems or puzzles, recognise
  simple patterns and relationships, generalise and
  predict. Suggest extensions by asking 'What if . . . ?'
  or 'What could I try next?'

- Explain how a problem was solved orally and,
  where appropriate, in writing.

Differentiation

The activity on Textbook pages 4 and 5 is for the
whole class, with differentiation by outcome.

Introducing the problem

Ask children to look at Textbook page 5, which has a
large grid to take cubes. Explain that you would like
them to use just enough cubes to make a square frame
in which one side uses 3 cubes. Then explain that you
would like them to take the cubes apart to make 4
equal lengths. Now ask:

- How many cubes did you use altogether?

- When you took the cubes apart, how many were there in
  each length? (2)

- Can you think of a way of recording what you have done
  so far?

Ask them to do the same for squares with sides of
4, 5, 6, . . . cubes.

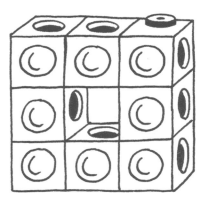

Teacher focus for activity

All abilities: Encourage children to draw each frame
they make, so that they can refer back to these if they
need to.

More able: Children should spot the patterns and
record their work in a way that allows them to make
predictions about larger-sized squares.

Average: Children may need some suggestions about
how to record systematically. They should spot the
'increase by 1' patterns and will probably see the
'increase by 4' patterns. A systematic means of
recording would be with numbers in a table, such as
the following:

Cubes along each side	Cubes in each length	Total number of cubes used
3	2	8
4	3	12
5	4	16

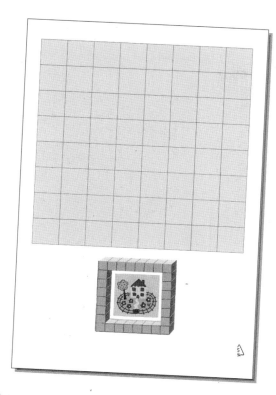

Less able: Children should be able to build the squares and, with help, find how many cubes are in each length. They will probably need help with recording in a systematic way so that they can see the 'increase by 1' patterns.

Some questions to ask as children work include:

- *How many cubes were there in one length? And altogether? Can you think of a connection between those numbers?*
- *Suppose you made a frame with sides of 9 cubes. How many cubes would be in one length? How many would be used altogether? How did you work that out?*
- *What if the frame had a side of 12 cubes: what could you tell me about that? How did you work that out?*

Optional adult input

Work with the Less able group. Ask each child to make the frame and then together make a group record of what has been done. Ask questions such as: *How many cubes in each length / altogether? What patterns can you see in the numbers we have recorded?*

Plenary

1 The solutions to these square frames can be predicted most easily where children have recorded their answers systematically and in table form. As you take feedback from children, begin by asking children from each group to discuss their findings. Give encouragement and praise as they explain how they solved the problem.

2 Discuss how children recorded their findings.

Invite children to explain what and how they recorded their results. Now ask:

- *Which method of recording works well?*
- *Why do you think that is the best method of recording?*

3 On the board, write the headings for the table as shown in **Solutions**. Invite children to write in each solution for squares with sides of 3, 4, 5 and 6 cubes. Ask:

- *What patterns can you see in the first column?* (increase by 1 each time)
- *What about the next column, which shows how many cubes in each length: what pattern can you see there?* (1 less than the cubes on each side, with an increase of 1 each time)
- *Now, what do you notice about the total number of cubes used: what pattern can you see?* (4 times the cubes in each length; pattern increases by 4 each time)
- *So, what should we write for a frame of 7 . . . 8 . . . 9 . . . 10? And what should we write for the cubes in each length? How many cubes would we use altogether for each frame?*

As the table is being completed, children may find it helpful to use their cubes on the grid in the Textbook and to try out each frame. Suggest this after children have predicted the numbers to go into the table each time.

Development

Encourage children to consider how they might change the problem. Suggestions might include making rectangles or other shapes, such as triangles. Check that they keep the increase in size of their shape logical. For example, for rectangles they could keep 2 sides the same length each time and just increase the other sides by 1 cube. (See **Useful mathematical information**, page 82.)

Solutions

Cubes along each side	Cubes in each length	Total number of cubes used
3	2	8
4	3	12
5	4	16
6	5	20
7	6	24
8	7	28
9	8	32
10	9	36
11	10	40
12	11	44

2 Number line

Minimum prior experience

counting to 100 and beyond; place value

Resources

paper for recording, 1–100 number line (PCMs 1 and 2),
PCM 3 Hundred square, Textbook page 6

Key vocabulary

count in 1s, more, less, tally, relationship, 1-, 2-, and 3-digit
number, approximate, unit, approximately, method, jotting, puzzle,
pattern

2 Number line

The children in Class 2 made a number line from 1 to 100.
They cut out each digit separately.
To make the number 21, the children cut out a [2] and a [1].
How many of each digit did they have to cut out to make the number line?

*Count all the 1s.
Now what about the 2s?
Now count the 3s.
Can you guess the others?*

What's the problem?

The numbers 1 to 100 include 1-, 2- and 3-digit
numbers. Children are asked to find out how many of
each digit is needed to make all of the numbers from
1 to 100.

Problem solving objectives

- Solve mathematical problems or puzzles, recognise
  simple patterns and relationships, generalise and
  predict. Suggest extensions by asking *'What if . . . ?'*
  or *'What could I try next?'*

- Explain how a problem was solved orally and,
  where appropriate, in writing.

Differentiation

The activity on Textbook page 6 is for the whole class,
with differentiation by outcome.

Introducing the problem

Explain the problem to the children: *Each number from
1 to 100 has 1, 2 or 3 digits in it. Tell me some 1-digit, 2-digit
and 3-digit numbers.* Pause and give children time to
respond. Write their suggestions on the board, in
numerals. *What different digits are used to make up all the
numbers?* (Elicit the digits 1 to 9)

*A class wanted to make its own number line from 1 to 100,
cutting out all of the digits separately. I wonder how many
1s, 2s, 3s, and so on, they needed.*

Check that children understand what they have to do.
Explain that you are really interested in how they
solve the problem.

Teacher focus for activity

All abilities: Check that children understand how to
tally. If necessary, show them how to make tally
marks and explain how these can be counted in 5s.
Encourage all children to estimate how many of each
digit they think there will be and to write this down.

This represents 5 and 3, which make 8.

More able: Discourage children from using the 100
square, as they should think about the use of the
digits, rather than just counting them. If they need
help with recording, suggest that they make a simple
table. They may find it helpful to write all the
numbers with a 1, then all the numbers with a 2, and
so on.

Average and Less able: Children may benefit from
using a 100 square or number line so that they have a
visual reminder for each number. They may find it
helpful to tally for each number, so they will need to
make a clear list of digits, then put tallies against
them.

Ask questions as children work, such as:

- *What have you done so far?*
- *Can you see any patterns?*
- *How many do you think there will be? Why is that?*

Optional adult input

Work with the Less able group, helping them to tally accurately.

Plenary

1 Begin by asking children about their estimates:

- *Approximately how many '1's did you think there would be?*

- *Why did you think that?*

- *Did you think that all the numbers would be the same? Why did you think that?*

2 Now invite various children to explain how they worked out their solutions. Their answers may include:

- Counting all the '1's, then the '2's, and so on, using a 100 square to help.

- Tallying for each number, and making a list of results.

- Working out 2 or 3 solutions, then guessing that the others would be the same.

Ask questions about their solutions:

- *What do you notice about your results? What patterns can you see?*

- *Which digits are different? Why is that?*

3 Write the numbers 1 to 9 on the board. Discuss with children that these are single-digit numbers, or 'units', and that they have no digit in the tens column. Rewrite these digits, but this time put a 0 in the tens column: 01, 02, 03, . . . Ask:

- *If we rewrote these numbers with a zero in the tens column, how many zeros would there be?*

- *And how many zeros would there then be altogether?* (See **Useful mathematical information**, page 82.)

- *What about the digit '1'?*

If children are unable to explain, tell them that there is an extra '1' needed to write 100.

4 Invite pairs to explain how they recorded their work. Discuss the different methods used, such as keeping tallies and counting, marking digits on the 100 square as they were counted. Ask children which methods were the easiest to understand.

Congratulate children on successfully solving this problem.

Development

What if a 0–99 square were used instead of a 1–100 square? (There would be 20 of each digit 1–9, and 10 zero digits.)

Solutions

Digit	How many needed	Numbers
0	11	10, 20, 30, 40, 50, 60, 70, 80, 90, 100
1	21	1, 10, 11, 12, 13, 14, 15, 16, 17, 18, 19, 21, 31, 41, 51, 61, 71, 81, 91, 100
2	20	2, 12, 20, 21, 22, 23, 24, 25, 26, 27, 28, 29, 32, 42, 52, 62, 72, 82, 92
3	20	3, 13, 23, 30, 31, 32, 33, 34, 35, 36, 37, 38, 39, 43, 53, 63, 73, 83, 93
4	20	4, 14, 24, 34, 40, 41, 42, 43, 44, 45, 46, 47, 48, 49, 54, 64, 74, 84, 94
5	20	5, 15, 25, 35, 45, 50, 51, 52, 53, 54, 55, 56, 57, 58, 59, 65, 75, 85, 95
6	20	6, 16, 26, 36, 46, 56, 60, 61, 62, 63, 64, 65, 66, 67, 68, 69, 76, 86, 96
7	20	7, 17, 27, 37, 47, 57, 67, 70, 71, 72, 73, 74, 75, 76, 77, 78, 79, 87, 97
8	20	8, 18, 28, 38, 48, 58, 68, 78, 80, 81, 82, 83, 84, 85, 86, 87, 88, 89, 98
9	20	9, 19, 29, 39, 49, 59, 69, 79, 89, 90, 91, 92, 93, 94, 95, 96, 97, 98, 99

3 How old is Granny?

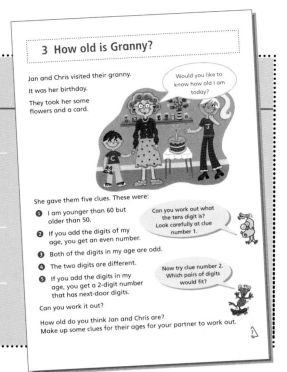

Minimum prior experience

investigating simple properties of numbers to 100; odd and even numbers

Resources

Textbook page 7, PCM 18, PCM 4 Digit cards, paper

Key vocabulary

digit, puzzle, odd, even, 1- or 2-digit number, tens, units, between, explain how you got your answer

What's the problem?

Children use what they know about place value and odd and even numbers to find an unknown number.

Problem solving objectives

- Investigate a general statement about familiar numbers by finding examples that satisfy it.
- Explain how a problem was solved orally, and where appropriate, in writing.

Differentiation

This activity is differentiated by outcome and resources.

Less able: PCM 18 can be used as a simplified version of Textbook page 7

Introducing the problem

Explain the problem: *Granny decided to tell her grandchildren how old she was. Instead of just saying her age, she set them a puzzle.* Read through the puzzle on Textbook page 7 together.

Discuss the word 'digit', as a number in another number. Write the number 35 on the board and ask:

- *Which is the tens/units digit?*
- *Can you tell me a number that has a 4 as the tens digit?*

Explain that you are interested in how children work out the puzzle and in how they record their work. Ask them to begin the puzzle immediately, working with their partner.

Teacher focus for activity

All abilities: This activity involves using what children know about number properties, including:

- pairs of single-digit numbers that total an even number;
- pairs of single-digit odd numbers that total an even number;
- understanding that consecutive numbers (called next-door numbers in the activity) are in counting order.

More able: Encourage children to read through all of the problem and to discuss how many facts they need to explore. If they read clues 2 and 3 on Textbook page 7, they may realise that they are searching for pairs of odd numbers that make an even total. Encourage them to write down all that they find out.

Average and Less able: Children may benefit from using digit cards, so that they can follow their understanding of the clues with possible numbers in front of them. Encourage them to work through each clue and write down what they find out.

Ask questions as children work, for example:

- *Which are the odd/even numbers? How do you know that?*
- *What totals can you make with odd numbers between 1 and 9?*
- *Give me an example of next-door numbers.*

Optional adult input

Work with the Less able group. This activity could be undertaken as a whole-group activity. Encourage children to demonstrate what each clue could mean using the digit cards.

Plenary

Invite children to explain how they set about solving the problem. Take each clue in turn.

The following works through the clues on Textbook page 7. The solution to PCM 18 is the same. However the clues are slightly different. (See Solutions.)

Clue 1: I am younger than 60 but older than 50. Ask:

- *What does this clue tell us about how old Granny is?*
- *So how old might Granny be?*

Elicit from children that Granny's age, just from this clue, lies between 51 and 59. Ask them to explain how they know that Granny cannot be 50 or 60 years old. (*Because Granny is between 50 and 60.*)

Clue 2: If you add the digits of my age you get an even number. Ask:

- *Which even numbers can we make by adding single-digit numbers?*

On the board, draw a table to show children's suggestions, e.g.:

2	$1 + 1$
4	$1 + 3, 2 + 2$
6	$1 + 5, 2 + 4, 3 + 3$
8	$1 + 7, 2 + 6, 3 + 5, 4 + 4$
10	$1 + 9, 2 + 8, 3 + 7, 4 + 6, 5 + 5$
12	$3 + 9, 4 + 8, 5 + 7, 6 + 6$
14	$5 + 9, 6 + 8, 7 + 7$
16	$7 + 9, 8 + 8$
18	$9 + 9$

Ask:

- *What do you notice about making even totals?*
- *What if you add two even/odd numbers?*
- *What if you add an odd and an even number? Is the total odd or even?* (odd)

Some children may be able to point out that by looking at clues 2 and 3 together they only need to consider even totals made from pairs of odd numbers. Remind children that by adding any pair of odd numbers the total is **always** even (and you can therefore solve the problem without clue 2). See **Useful mathematical information**, page 82, for more about totalling odd and even numbers.

Children may realise that they are looking only for numbers made by adding 5 to another odd number, because the tens digit must be 5.

Consider **clue 3**: Both of the digits in my age are odd. Ask children to suggest which numbers they should consider. They may need to be reminded about what they know from clue 1: that is, that Granny's age lies between 51 and 59. Make a list of possible ages that children suggest: 51, 53, 55, 57 and 59.

Ask: *Which of these ages can't it be, if we look at* **clue 4**? (55, because the digits are the same)

Now look at **clue 5**: If you add the digits in my age, you get a 2-digit number that has next-door digits. Check that children understand that next-door numbers in this instance refers to consecutive numbers. Ask children to total each pair of digits, and write the number sentences on the board:

$5 + 1 = 6$

$5 + 3 = 8$

$5 + 7 = 12$

$5 + 9 = 14$

Ask:

- *Can you see a 2-digit number with next-door digits?*
- *So, how old is Granny? Yes, she is 57 years old.*

Invite various children from each ability group to show how they recorded their results and their thinking. Encourage systematic working through the clues and explanation of thinking.

Development

Ask children to imagine what ages the 2 children illustrated in the Textbook might be and to make up some clues for each of their ages for a partner to work out.

Solutions

Granny is 57 years old.

PCM 18
Children narrow down the possible solutions until they reach 57.
1 51, 52, 53, 54, 55, 56, 57, 58, 59
2 51, 53, 55, 57, 59
3 51, 53, 57, 59
4 53, 57
5 57

4 Number generator

4 Number generator

❶ Choose any two digits from 1 to 9.
Find all the 2-digit numbers that you can make with these digits.
How many numbers can you make?

❷ Choose any three digits from 1 to 9.
Find all the 3-digit numbers that you can make with these digits.
How many numbers can you make?
Is it always this amount of numbers for three digits?

Have you tried making the numbers with digit cards?

Try writing your numbers in order, starting with the lowest.

Minimum prior experience

place value of 3-digit numbers for More able group and 2-digit numbers for Average and Less able groups

Resources

squared paper, plain paper, counters, digit cards 1–9 (PCM 4), 2-spike and 3-spike abacuses (PCM 5), Textbook page 8

Key vocabulary

number, one, two, three . . . one thousand, units, tens, hundreds, thousands, place value, compare, order

What's the problem?

Children explore how many different numbers they can make using the digits 1 to 9.

Problem solving objectives

- Solve mathematical problems or puzzles, recognise simple patterns and relationships, generalise and predict. Suggest extensions by asking 'What if . . . ?' or 'What could I try next?'
- Explain how a problem was solved orally and, where appropriate, in writing.

Differentiation

More able: Textbook page 8, problem 2. Children make 3-digit numbers.

Average and Less able: Textbook page 8, problem 1. Children make 2-digit numbers.

Introducing the problem

Explain the problem: *Look at the problem in your book. You are asked to choose some number digits, choosing from 1 to 9. How many different numbers can you make with your digits? What if you choose different digits: how many different numbers can you make now?*

Remind children that you are not just interested in their answers. You also want to know how they worked out the problem. Suggest to them that they think about how they are going to record their answers. They should now tackle the problem.

Teacher focus for activity

All abilities: Careful and accurate recording is important for this activity, as by recording their numbers they will be able to see how many numbers they have made. If they record systematically, from, say, smallest to largest number, they should be able to check that they have made all the possible numbers.

More able: Children may find it helpful to model the 3-digit numbers using a 3-spike abacus (PCM 5) and counters. Suggest to children that they try different arrangements of their chosen digits in order to find different 3-digit numbers.

Average and Less able: Where children need help, suggest that they model their numbers using a 2-spike abacus (PCM 5) and counters.

Ask questions as they work, such as:
- *Which digits did you choose? Which numbers have you made?*
- *How do you know that you have made all the numbers possible with those digits?*
- *If you choose different digits will you be able to make the same amount of numbers, or more or less numbers? How do you know?*

Optional adult input

Work with the Less able group. Children should all choose the same digits and find how many different numbers they can make. They can share their answers and make individual recordings.

Plenary

1 Ask children doing problem 1 to give some solutions. All of their responses should show 2 numbers. Ask children to read these numbers, and check that they recognise the difference between, for example, 18 and 81. Ask children to make a 2-digit number on a paper abacus using counters. Now ask them to make the other number using the same digits. Ask: *What do you notice?* Children may notice that it is the place value of the digits that changes the value of the number.

2 Ask children doing problem 2 to share some results. They should have found 6 different numbers each time. Write a set of these numbers on the board, such as, for 1, 3 and 5: 135, 153, 315, 351, 513 and 531. Ask everyone to read the numbers with you. Provide each child with a 3-spike abacus (PCM 5) and ask them to make all the numbers possible using 1, 3 and 5. Ask them what they notice.

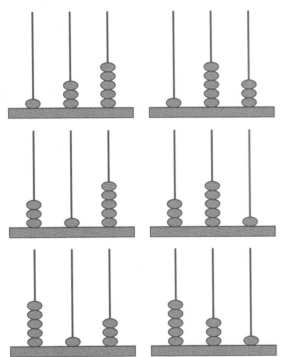

Ask:

- *What do you notice about these numbers?*

- *Are there any more numbers that we could make using these digits? Why not?*

- *Can you make some numbers using the digits 1, 4 and 6? Which numbers can you make? Can you put them in order starting with the lowest? How many numbers are there with a 1 in the hundreds? And a 1 in the tens? And a 1 in the units? What about the 4/6? Is it the same?* (146, 164, 416, 461, 614, 641)

3 Discuss how children recorded their results. Some children may have written lists that are in order starting with the lowest number. Discuss how this can help to check that all of the numbers have been found.

Development

More able children may want to try making numbers with 4 digits. They will need to work systematically if they are to be sure that they have found all of the possible solutions.

Solutions

For 2-digit numbers, where the digits are different, there are always 2 possible numbers that can be made: for example, for the digits 1 and 2, it is possible to make 12 and 21.

For 3-digit numbers, where each digit is different, there are always 6 possible numbers that can be made: for example, for the digits 1, 2 and 3, it is possible to make 123, 132, 213, 231, 312 and 321.

If zero were used, then this would alter the total of 2- or 3-digit numbers that can be made, because zero is not used to mark an empty tens or hundreds place in single-digit or 2-digit numbers.

See **Useful mathematical information**, page 83, for a discussion on the use of zeros in numbers.

5 Next-door numbers

Minimum prior experience

addition of small numbers

Resources

paper, a solution chart with 7 columns (to be used in the plenary, see **Solutions**), Textbook page 9, PCM 1 Number line, PCM 3 Hundred square, PCM 4 Digit cards

Key vocabulary

add, addition, more, plus, make, sum, total, altogether, equation, pattern, puzzle, calculate, method, jotting, answer

What's the problem?

Within their given number range, children explore numbers that can be made by totalling consecutive numbers.

Problem solving objectives

- Solve mathematical problems or puzzles, recognise simple patterns and relationships, generalise and predict. Suggest extensions by asking 'What if . . . ?' or 'What could I try next?'
- Choose and use appropriate operations and efficient calculation strategies to solve problems.
- Explain how a problem was solved orally and in writing.

Differentiation

More able: Textbook page 9, problem 3. Make numbers from 20 to 30.

Average: Textbook page 9, problem 2. Make numbers from 10 to 20.

Less able: Textbook page 9, problem 1. Make numbers from 0 to 10.

Introducing the problem

Say the problem to the children: *Sam and Chris noticed that some numbers can be made from next-door numbers.* On the board write:

$4 + 5 = 9$
$2 + 3 + 4 = 9$

Say: *It is possible to make 9 in 2 different ways by adding next-door numbers. Your task is to find other numbers that can be made by adding next-door numbers.*

Ask children to discuss the problem with their partner and to decide how they will tackle it and how they will record their findings, before beginning to tackle the problem.

Teacher focus for activity

All abilities: Children are likely to use a variety of methods to solve this problem – from a random search to a systematic approach. If children are unsure about recording, suggest to them that they record in number order and write addition sentences to show their answers. Some children may produce their own way of recording, which could include writing the target number, with the consecutive numbers written underneath.

More able: Children should solve this problem using mental methods and jottings. Encourage them to work systematically, starting with 20 and working on to 30.

Average: Children may find number lines helpful, because they can see the numbers in order.

Less able: Children may find using number cards and number lines helpful, because they can choose pairs of consecutive digit cards and calculate the totals.

Some questions to ask, as children work, include:

- *How did you work that out?*
- *Is there another way of making that number from next-door numbers?*

● *What if you added the next next-door number, what total would you make then?*

Optional adult input

Work with the More able group. Encourage them to search for more than one solution where possible, and to look for patterns in the results.

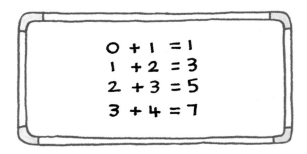

$$0 + 1 = 1$$
$$1 + 2 = 3$$
$$2 + 3 = 5$$
$$3 + 4 = 7$$

Plenary

1 Put up the solution chart and ask children to suggest solutions for each number. When the solutions for 1 to 10 have been written in, ask:

● *What patterns do you notice?*

Children may notice that odd numbers can always be made from the sum of 2 consecutive numbers. See **Useful mathematical information**, page 83, for why this is so.

Continued above right.

2 Now continue to write in solutions for 11 to 20. Ask:

● *If 7 equals 3 add 4, and 9 equals 4 add 5, what will 11 equal? And 13? . . .*

● *Can we write in one solution for all the odd numbers using what we already know?*

3 When the solutions for 21 to 30 have been completed, ask if there are any numbers that have more than one solution and write in these. Encourage children to use what they already have in order to find more solutions, for example, $15 = 1 + 2 + 3 + 4 + 5$, so what would be the number made by $1 + 2 + 3 + 4 + 5 + 6$?

4 Draw the children's attention to the numbers where there are no solutions (2, 4, 8 and 16). Ask:

● *What do you notice about these numbers?*

If children do not spot the pattern, point out that 4 is double 2, 8 is double 4 and 16 is double 8. Ask:

● *If this is a pattern, then what would the next number with no solution be?*

5 Discuss how 32 can be made by addition, and write on the board: $16 + 16$, $14 + 18$, $17 + 15$ . . . Point out that it is not possible to use consecutive numbers. (See **Useful mathematical information**, page 83, for further discussion about the sums of consecutive numbers.)

Development

Find solutions for numbers 31 to 40 . . .

Solutions

Total	Add 2 next-door numbers	Add 3 next-door numbers	Add 4 next-door numbers	Add 5 next-door numbers	Add 6 next-door numbers	Add 7 next-door numbers
1 =	0 + 1					
2 =						
3 =	1 + 2					
4 =						
5 =	2 + 3					
6 =		1 + 2 + 3				
7 =	3 + 4					
8 =						
9 =	4 + 5	2 + 3 + 4				
10 =			1 + 2 + 3 + 4			
11 =	5 + 6					
12 =		3 + 4 + 5				
13 =	6 + 7					
14 =			2 + 3 + 4 + 5			
15 =	7 + 8	4 + 5 + 6		1 + 2 + 3 + 4 + 5		
16 =						
17 =	8 + 9					
18 =		5 + 6 + 7	3 + 4 + 5 + 6			
19 =	9 + 10					
20 =				2 + 3 + 4 + 5 + 6		
21 =	10 + 11	6 + 7 + 8			1 + 2 + 3 + 4 + 5 + 6	
22 =			4 + 5 + 6 + 7			
23 =	11 + 12					
24 =		7 + 8 + 9				
25 =	12 + 13			3 + 4 + 5 + 6 + 7		
26 =			5 + 6 + 7 + 8			
27 =	13 + 14	8 + 9 + 10			2 + 3 + 4 + 5 + 6 + 7	
28 =						1 + 2 + 3 + 4 + 5 + 6 + 7
29 =	14 + 15					
30 =		9 + 10 + 11	6 + 7 + 8 + 9	4 + 5 + 6 + 7 + 8		

6 What's the rule?

What's the problem?

Children identify number sorting rules, using properties of numbers such as odd numbers or multiples of 5.

Problem solving objectives

- Solve mathematical problems or puzzles, recognise simple patterns and relationships, generalise and predict.

- Investigate a general statement about familiar numbers by finding examples that satisfy it.

Differentiation

All children work from Textbook pages 10 and 11. Vary the range of number cards given to each group:

More able: Numbers 50 to 100.

Average: Numbers 0 to 50.

Less able: Numbers 0 to 30.

Introducing the problem

On the board, draw a circle. Explain to children that you are thinking of a rule for sorting numbers and will write the numbers that fit your sorting rule inside the circle. Write 5, 10 and 15 inside the circle and 3, 8 and 11 outside the circle. Hopefully by now there should be hands up, with children recognising that the rule is multiples of 5.

Explain the puzzle to the children: *Some sorting rules are written on the stones around the Textbook page. The one whose turn it is secretly chooses a rule and starts to put the*

number cards onto the picture in their book. The cards that follow the rule go into the pond; put the others outside the pond. Now your partner has to guess which rule you've chosen. Keep putting down cards until their guess is correct. Decide how you are going to record what you have done. Then swap over.

Teacher focus for activity

More able: Encourage children to think up their own sorting rules, instead of using the stones. Challenge children to find as many different rules as they can in the given time, and to record each one quickly and efficiently.

Average and Less able: If children are unsure, choose a rule, such as 'numbers greater than 20', and start putting the cards down, sorting into greater than and not greater than 20. When children are confident, they can try this again for themselves, choosing another rule. Encourage children to put numbers in order, as a way of checking.

As children work, ask questions such as:

- *Can you tell me some more numbers that fit this rule?*
- *Can you tell me some numbers that don't fit this rule? How do you know?*
- (Said in a whisper to one child of a pair) *What other rules could you try?*

Optional adult input

Work with the Less able group. Lay all the number cards out in order and choose one of the sorting rules. Take cards that fit the rule in order, placing them in the pond, so that children recognise, for

Put cards that fit the rule into the pond.

Put other cards outside.

Can your partner guess the sorting rule?

Record what you have done.

Now your partner chooses a rule.

Think of your own sorting rule to try.

even numbers

multiples of 5

multiples of 10

numbers between 10 and 20

multiples of 3

example, that you are taking every other number. Ask children: *What would come next? . . . and next? How do you know that?* When children have identified your rule, they take turns to choose one of their own.

Plenary

1 On the board, draw a large circle. Ask children from each ability group to choose one of their puzzles to set for the rest of the class. Children write some numbers on the board, choosing whether to put the number inside or outside the circle, depending upon whether or not it fits the rule. Invite the other children to guess what the rule is. If children have difficulty guessing the rule, say:

   ● *What other numbers do you think will go inside the circle? Why do you think that?*

   ● *What numbers could go outside the circle? How do you know that?*

2 When children have guessed the rule, say:

   ● *Give me a number that definitely does not fit the rule. How do you know that?*

3 Discuss how children decided to record their rules. Recording could include:

   ● Lists of numbers that fit/do not fit the rule.

   ● Drawings of the circle with numbers inside/outside it.

   ● Simple 2-column tables: one column for the rule numbers, one for numbers outside.

4 Invite children to show examples of recording and to explain why they chose their method. Ask children about the different ways of recording: What do they like? What could be improved? Suggest to them that the best ways of recording make it easy for others to see what the rules are: for example, where numbers have been ordered it is easier to spot the rule. However, when playing the game, the More able group may have deliberately chosen cards in a seemingly random way in order to confuse their partner. It may be helpful if they order numbers when they record them, as a check.

Solutions

Below is a list of possible rules or number facts that children might use. It is by no means an exhaustive list.

● Multiples, for example:

Fits the rule	Doesn't fit the rule
(2s) 2, 4, 6, 8 . . .	1, 3, 5, 7 . . .
(5s) 5, 10, 15 . . .	2, 4, 6 . . .
(10s) 10, 20, 30 . . .	3, 5, 12 . . .
(3s) 3, 6, 9, 12 . . .	2, 4, 11, 19 . . .

● Odd and even numbers.

● Numbers that are more/less than given numbers. (See **Useful mathematical information**, page 83, for further details.) For example:

Fits the rule	Doesn't fit the rule
(Greater than 40) 45, 56, 89, 65 . . .	13, 33, 39, 40 . . .
(Less than 25) 1, 2, 3, 4, 5 . . . 24	25, 26, 27, 28, 29 . . .

7 Fraction flags

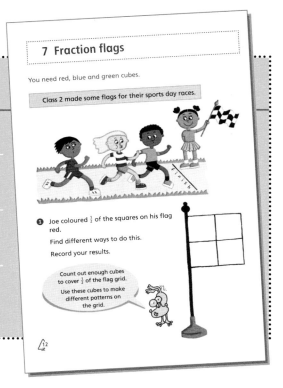

Minimum prior experience

finding fractions of quantities

Resources

interlocking cubes, Textbook pages 12 and 13, PCM 6, PCM 7

Key vocabulary

part, equal parts, fraction, quarter, third, half

What's the problem?

Children investigate different ways of finding a given fraction of a rectangular grid.

Problem solving objectives

- Solve mathematical problems or puzzles, recognise simple patterns and relationships, generalise and predict. Suggest extensions by asking 'What if . . . ?' or 'What could I try next?'
- Choose and use appropriate operations and efficient calculation strategies to solve problems.
- Explain how a problem was solved orally and, where appropriate, in writing.

Differentiation

More able: Textbook pages 12–13, problem 3.
Find one third of 12.

Average: Textbook pages 12–13, problem 2.
Find one quarter of 8.

Less able: Textbook pages 12–13, problem 1.
Find one half of 4.

Introducing the problem

Ask children to look at the grids in the Textbook. Explain which grid is for which group, then explain the problem: *Some children made Sports Day flags by colouring a fraction of a grid. There are different ways of making the fractions they coloured. How many different ways can you find? Don't forget to record your work.* Remind children that they can use PCM 6 or PCM 7 to record each attempt.

Ask children to talk in their pairs about how they will solve the problem before they begin.

Teacher focus for activity

All abilities: When recording their work, children should use PCM 6 or PCM 7 to draw their results. As children work, suggest to them that pairs join up with other pairs to compare their results, so that, between them, they find as many different solutions as possible.

More able: If children are unsure about finding one third of 12, suggest to them that they find it by sharing out 12 cubes into 3 piles.

Average and Less able: When children have difficulty, ask: *How many squares do you need to cover?* Say: *Try counting out that number of cubes and placing them onto the grid. Now, can you find different ways of doing that?*

As children work, ask questions, such as:

- *How many cubes do you need to cover $\frac{1}{2}$, $\frac{1}{4}$, $\frac{1}{3}$?*
- *What if you move those cubes? Can you place them in a different way? Does that change what fraction of the grid is covered?* (No, because the same number of squares are still covered.)

Optional adult input

Work with the More able group. Ask children to record their responses quickly onto PCM 7 and to look for another arrangement. After 10 minutes, ask children to compare results and see if they can spot further arrangements.

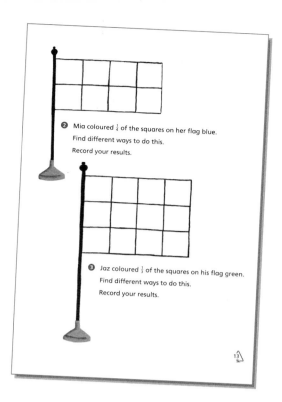

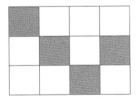

Some of the arrangements that children find may be translations, reflections or rotations of another arrangement. Discuss the arrangements found with children and ask for their opinion of whether these are the same or not. Demonstrate turning one arrangement through a right angle to make another. (See **Useful mathematical information**, page 83, for further discussion.)

Solutions

One half of 4 is any arrangement that shows 2 squares coloured, so the following are possibilities:

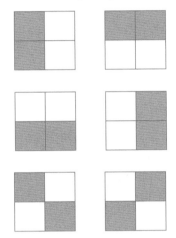

One quarter of 8 is any arrangement that shows 2 squares coloured, e.g.:

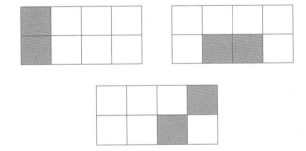

One third of 12 is any arrangement that shows 4 squares coloured, so any of the following would be acceptable, and, of course, there are many more possibilities:

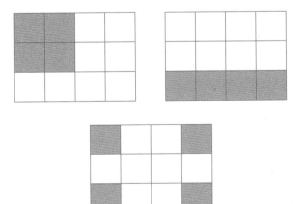

Plenary

1 Ask children from each group to show some of their responses. Discuss with children how, for example, $\frac{1}{2}$, $\frac{1}{4}$, or $\frac{1}{3}$ of the squares can be covered without all the cubes being together.

As well as perceiving this as half of a shape, it is also half of a quantity of squares.

2 Ask for responses for a $\frac{1}{2}$, a $\frac{1}{4}$ and a $\frac{1}{3}$, where the cubes are not together. Discuss how this is still a $\frac{1}{2}$, a $\frac{1}{4}$ or a $\frac{1}{3}$ of the total number of squares, and how it covers a $\frac{1}{2}$, a $\frac{1}{4}$ or a $\frac{1}{3}$ of the rectangle.

3 Encourage children to see that the same arrangement of cubes can be placed in different ways on the grid. Similarly, they can make reflections of the arrangement.

Ask: *Can you suggest other ways that we can make new arrangements?*

The answers can be as simple as 'move that one cube from here to there'.

8 Dart totals

Minimum prior experience

totalling 1- and 2-digit numbers

Resources

paper clips, base 10 apparatus, 0–20 number cards, Textbook pages 14 and 15, 0–50 and 0–100 number lines (PCMs 1 and 2), PCM 3 Hundred square, PCM 8

Key vocabulary

add, plus, altogether, pattern, calculate, method, jotting, answer, number sentence, total, score

8 Dart totals

You need paper clips.

❶ Use 2 paper clips on the dartboard.
Find a way to make a total of 15.
Write this as a sum.
Now find different ways to make the total 15.
Try this again for totals of 16, 17 and 18.

❷ Use 3 paper clips on the dartboard each time.
Find as many ways of making a total of 20 as you can.
Now choose a total greater than 20. Find as many ways of making it as you can.
Do this again for another number.
What do you notice about your answers?
Record what you have done.

14

What's the problem?

Children find different ways of making totals from numbers 1 to 20.

Problem solving objectives

- Choose and use appropriate operations and efficient calculation strategies to solve problems.

- Solve mathematical problems or puzzles, recognise simple patterns and relationships, generalise and predict. Suggest extensions by asking 'What if . . .?' or 'What could I try next?'

- Explain how a problem was solved orally and, where appropriate, in writing.

Differentiation

More able: Textbook pages 14–15, problem 3. Use 3 numbers to total 50 or more.

Average: Textbook pages 14–15, problem 2. Use 3 numbers to total 20 or more.

Less able: Textbook pages 14–15, problem 1. Use 2 numbers to total 15 or more.

Introducing the problem

Explain the problem to children: *Use the paper clips to represent darts. Find different ways to make the total using all your darts each time.* Ask children to discuss how they will tackle the problem with their partner.

Remind children to record each turn using their own method and tell them that you will be interested to see how they do this. Point out that PCM 8 is available if they want to record the position of their darts.

Teacher focus for activity

All abilities: Children should use informal methods of calculation, involving knowledge about number bonds, and mental and pencil-and-paper calculation methods. Ask: *What number patterns can you see? Can you explain what is happening?*

More able: Encourage children to use mental methods when possible to work out their calculations. When they need help, show them the empty number line method for addition. For example, for 20 + 17 + 13, children could do 20 + 10 + 10 + 7 + 3:

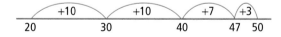

Ask questions such as: *What if one of your darts landed on number 7: could you still score 50 when you throw the other two darts? Why not?*

Average: Children should use mental methods, as well as pencil-and-paper methods. They may find the 100 square or number line helpful for counting on from a given number.

Less able: To simplify the problem, children use just 2-dart scores. Children can use resources to help them calculate, including base 10 apparatus and number cards.

❸ Use 3 paper clips on the dartboard each time.

Find as many ways of making a total of 50 as you can.

Now choose a total greater than 50. Find as many ways of making it as you can.

Do this again for another number.

What do you notice about your answers?

Record what you have done. Write about what you have found out.

Optional adult input

Work with the Less able group. Children take it in turns to suggest how to make the given total, using their chosen resources to help them, including mental methods. Discuss how they should record, and then make a group record of work done.

Plenary

1   Invite individuals to give totals for 50 and write these on the board, ordering them as shown in **Solutions**. Ask:

- *What pattern can you see?* (One number decreases by 1, while the other increases by 1 each time.)

- *Should we count 20 + 19 + 11 and 11 + 19 + 20? Why do you think that?*

Discuss how addition can be done in any order, so that, for example, 20 + 19 + 11 is the same as 11 + 19 + 20 or 19 + 11 + 20 . . . See **Useful mathematical information**, page 84, for further information about associativity and commutativity.

Talk about the number of solutions that can be found for 50. Ask: *How did you know that there were no more solutions? What did the number patterns tell you?* Encourage children to see that when all of the addition totals have been found, any others are repeats of what has already been found but with the numbers in a different order.

2   Write the solutions for 15 on the board in order (see **Solutions**). Ask:

- *What do you notice about these solutions?*

Discuss how, as 1 dart increases by 1, the other decreases by 1. Ask:

- *With 2 darts, what is the greatest total you can make?*

3   Repeat this for totals for 20 using 3 darts. Invite children to explain the pattern. Again, as 1 dart increases by 1, another must decrease by 1.

4   Ask children:

- *What is the largest total you can make with 3 darts?* (60) *Why can't you make a total larger than 60?*

- *What is the smallest total you can make with 3 darts?* (3)

5   Discuss which ways of recording make the number patterns clear. What is needed is a systematic recording, as the solutions show.

Solutions

50 can be made in the following ways:

20 + 20 + 10	19 + 18 + 13
20 + 19 + 11	19 + 17 + 14
20 + 18 + 12	19 + 16 + 15
20 + 17 + 13	18 + 18 + 14
20 + 16 + 14	18 + 17 + 15
20 + 15 + 15	18 + 16 + 16
19 + 19 + 12	17 + 17 + 16

Other solutions will be different orderings of the above.

It is possible to make totals, in the same way, up to 60. The possible number of solutions diminishes to one solution only for 60: 20 + 20 + 20

There are 33 ways of making 20 using 3 numbers each time, for example:

18 + 1 + 1
17 + 2 + 1
16 + 3 + 1 . . .

15 can be made with 2 numbers as follows:

1 + 14	5 + 10
2 + 13	6 + 9
3 + 12	7 + 8
4 + 11	

9 Arithmagons

Minimum prior experience

addition combinations for numbers below 10

Resources

counters with digits 1 to 6 on for each child/pair, paper, Textbook pages 16 and 17, 0–50 number line (PCM 1), PCM 9

Key vocabulary

add, more, plus, make, sum, total, altogether, mental calculation, method, jotting

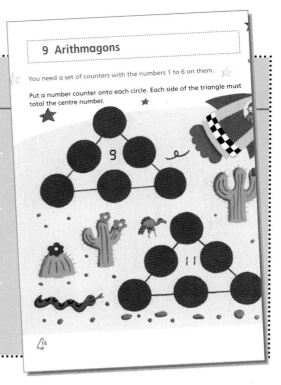

9 Arithmagons

You need a set of counters with the numbers 1 to 6 on them.

Put a number counter onto each circle. Each side of the triangle must total the centre number.

What's the problem?

Each arithmagon must have a given total for each side, using 3 numbers chosen from 1 to 6, and with all 6 numbers used for each problem.

Problem solving objectives

- Choose and use appropriate operations and efficient calculation strategies to solve problems.
- Solve mathematical problems or puzzles, recognise simple patterns and relationships, generalise and predict. Suggest extensions by asking 'What if . . . ?' or 'What could I try next?'
- Explain how a problem was solved orally and, where appropriate, in writing.

Differentiation

The activity on Textbook pages 16 and 17 is for the whole class; differentiation is by outcome and the resources used. Some children may find just one solution to each arithmagon, although expect the more able to search for more.

Introducing the problem

Set the problem: *These triangles are called arithmagons. Arrange your number counters on the first arithmagon so that the total of each side of the triangle is 9. Can you find more than one way of doing this? Look carefully at your results. What do you notice?*

Remind children that they can choose their own method of recording and that you will be interested in the different ways in which they tackle the problem.

Teacher focus for activity

All abilities: Encourage children to search for more than one solution.

More able and Average: Encourage children to work mentally to total the numbers.

Less able: Children may find it helpful to make jottings if they find the addition difficult. If needed, write one or more numbers onto each arithmagon on PCM 9, using the solutions on page 39, to give a starting point.

Children may find it difficult to see any link between, for example, solutions for 9 and solutions for 11. If they are stuck, encourage them to look at how to combine 3 numbers to make an odd total, and similarly for an even total.

Questions to ask as children work include:
- *What do you notice about the arrangement of numbers used to make 9/10/11/12?*
- *How did you work out your answers?*
- *From your results so far, can you work out another solution? How could you do that?*

Optional adult input

Work with the Most able group. Encourage each pair to find a range of different solutions and to record their results and what they notice in a systematic way.

Plenary

1   There is only one solution to each of the arithmagons, so where children have more than one, it will be a different arrangement of the same numbers. Invite children to write their solution to the 9 puzzle on the board. Ask:

*   *What do you notice about the corner numbers?*

*   *What do you notice about the numbers on each side of the arithmagon?*

2   Compare the corner numbers and the odd/even arrangements for each side for each of the solutions. They can also compare these with the total; for example, are the arrangements different if there is an odd total from when there is an even total? Ask:

*   *When totalling 3 numbers, what mixture of odd and even numbers makes an odd total?*

Discuss how odd totals can be made with:

odd + odd + odd, e.g. 3 + 5 + 1 = 9
even + even + odd, e.g. 2 + 6 + 1 = 9

Now discuss how an even total can be made:

even + even + even, e.g. 2 + 4 + 6 = 10
odd + odd + even, e.g. 3 + 5 + 2 = 10

Invite children to put this into a general sentence.

3   Ask: *How did you work out your answers?*

Some children may have worked out combinations to make the given total and then have found a way of placing that onto the arithmagon. Others may have found the solutions by trial and improvement.

4   Ask children to compare their recording with what others did. Ask them to decide which method of recording they preferred and to explain why.

For the 10 puzzle, ask:

*   *Can you have 3 odd numbers that add up to 10?*

*   *Which sets of 3 numbers will make 10?*

Discuss the 12 total.

Development

Would it be possible to have a total of 13, using the numbers 1 to 6? (The largest numbers are already the corner numbers. 12 is the largest total that can be made with the numbers 1 to 6 for an arithmagon.)

Solutions

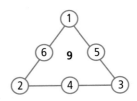

1, 5, 3
3, 4, 2   Side numbers are odd, odd, odd;
2, 6, 1   odd, even, even; and even, even, odd.

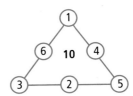

1, 4, 5
5, 2, 3   Side numbers are odd, even, odd for each side.
3, 6, 1

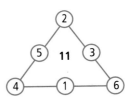

2, 3, 6
6, 1, 4   Side numbers are even, odd, even for each side.
4, 5, 2

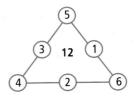

5, 1, 6   Side numbers are odd, odd, even;
6, 2, 4   even, even, even; and even, odd, odd.
4, 3, 5

See **Useful mathematical information**, page 84, for another way of using arithmagons.

10 Four in a row

Minimum prior experience

finding differences

Resources

counters in 2 colours, 2 colours of board markers or chalk, Textbook pages 18 and 19, PCM 1 Number lines, PCM 3 Hundred square, PCM 4 Digit cards, PCM 10

Key vocabulary

difference between, calculate, method, jotting, answer, right, wrong, correct, number sentence, equation

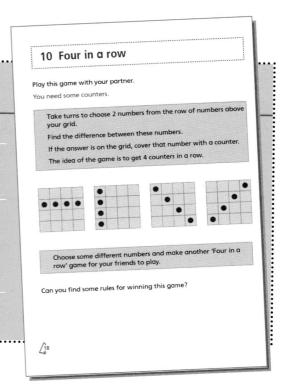

What's the problem?

The problem involves finding differences between pairs of numbers.

Problem solving objectives

- Choose and use appropriate operations and efficient calculation strategies to solve problems.
- Explain how the problem was solved orally and, where appropriate, in writing.

Differentiation

More able: Textbook pages 18–19, problem 3. Use numbers between 14 and 50.

Average: Textbook pages 18–19, problem 2. Use numbers between 4 and 25.

Less able: Textbook pages 18–19, problem 1. Use numbers between 1 and 20.

Introducing the problem

Ask children to look at the grids on Textbook page 19. Explain the game: *You will each need some counters. Take turns to choose 2 numbers from the row of numbers above the grid and find the difference between these numbers. If the answer is on the grid, cover that number with a counter. The idea of the game is to get 4 counters in a row.*

Make it clear to children that you are interested in how they work out the answers and how they tackle the problem. Encourage children to think about winning strategies.

Teacher focus for activity

All abilities: The activity encourages children to work mentally to find the difference between pairs of numbers. As children work, ask them to explain how they will try to win the game: *Why did you choose that pair of numbers?*

More able: Children may need to make jottings to work out the differences or use the 100 square. Decide whether to show children how to use an empty number line for this.

The difference between 34 and 50 is 16. (See **Useful mathematical information**, page 84, for further details about using empty number lines.)

Average: Children may need resources to help them to find differences, e.g. a number line or 100 square. Ask: *How did you work out the difference between those numbers?*

Less able: Children may just choose pairs of numbers where they already know the difference. This will lead to a random approach to the game and will make winning more difficult. Encourage children to look at the grid and decide which square they need to cover next – either to win or to stop their partner from winning. They can then work out differences, using mental methods, resources or both, to find the solution that they need.

Give the children hints:

- *Which pair of numbers do you think will give that difference?*

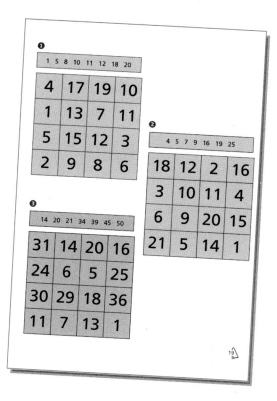

❶
| 1 | 5 | 8 | 10 | 11 | 12 | 18 | 20 |

4	17	19	10
1	13	7	11
5	15	12	3
2	9	8	6

❷
| 4 | 5 | 7 | 9 | 16 | 19 | 25 |

18	12	2	16
3	10	11	4
6	9	20	15
21	5	14	1

❸
| 14 | 20 | 21 | 34 | 39 | 45 | 50 |

31	14	20	16
24	6	5	25
30	29	18	36
11	7	13	1

- *How did you work that out?*
- *Which square do you need to cover to stop your partner from winning?*

Optional adult input

Work with the Average group, checking that they are thinking about winning strategies, such as blocking squares that their partner might need.

Plenary

1   Invite various children to explain how they played the game. Discuss the strategies they used, such as:

- blocking their partner's next move by covering that square
- covering squares that do not make a line in order to give different possibilities for future moves

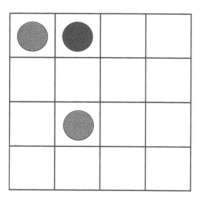

- thinking ahead by trying to block future moves and looking for opportunities to develop possible future moves.

Many children will have already played the counter game, or the computer version of it, and will have some ideas about winning strategies. Discuss these as a class.

2   On the board, draw one of the grids from the Textbook. Divide the class into 2 groups to play against each other. Choose a child from each group to mark the chosen solution onto the board each time. When either group has won, or the teams have reached stalemate, invite children to explain their thinking as they played the game. Ask:

- *Why did you choose this square?*
- *How could you stop the other side from winning?*
- *How did you work out which numbers to use so that you could cover this square?*
- *Did you find any differences that were not on the grid? What did you do about those numbers? (This applies to grids 2 and 3 only.)*

Choose another grid and play again. Encourage children to think about the strategies that they could use in order to win.

3   Where children have difficulty finding the differences, revise how this can be done, e.g. by complementary addition: *To find the difference between 19 and 5, work out how many more you need to add to 5 to get 19. Begin with 5. Add on 10 to make 15, then 4 more to make 19. So the difference between 19 and 5 is 10 add 4, which is 14.* Repeat for two of the numbers in the problems, e.g. 34 and 50.

Development

Children make another 'Four in a row' game to play with their friends and family, using PCM 10 and choosing different numbers.

Solutions

All the differences on the grids can be made with the numbers listed for each, with the following exceptions:

Grid 2:   The difference between 16 and 9 is 7, which is not on the grid.

Grid 3:   The difference between 20 and 39 is 19, which is not on the grid.

11 Square numbers

Minimum prior experience	
addition of 2 numbers crossing 10s boundaries	
Resources	
class 100 square, marker pen, counters, plain paper for recording, Textbook page 20, PCMs 1 and 2 Number lines and PCM 3 Hundred square	
Key vocabulary	
add, more, plus, make, sum, total, altogether, pattern, calculation, method, diagonal, opposite	

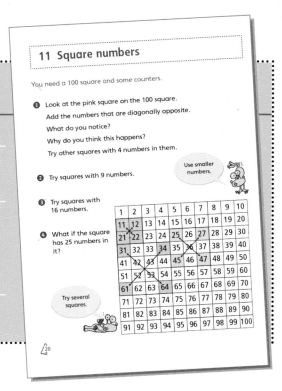

What's the problem?

Using addition, children investigate whether the total of diagonally opposite numbers in squares of numbers on a 100 square will always be the same.

Problem solving objectives

● Investigate a general statement about familiar numbers or shapes by finding examples that satisfy it.

● Solve mathematical problems or puzzles, recognise simple patterns and relationships, generalise and predict. Suggest extensions by asking 'What if . . . ?' or 'What could I try next?'

Differentiation

More able: Textbook page 20, problems 1 to 4. Investigate squares with 4, 9 and 16 numbers.

Average: Textbook page 20, problems 1 to 3. Investigate squares with 4 and 9 numbers.

Less able: Textbook page 20, problems 1 and 2. Investigate squares with 4 numbers.

Introducing the problem

Say the problem: *Look at the 100 square in your textbook. Look at the small pink square with opposite numbers of 11 and 22, then 12 and 21. What happens if you total each of these pairs of diagonally opposite numbers?* (The total is 33 each time.) Discuss quickly what is meant by 'diagonally opposite'. *What if you choose a different square? What do you notice? Use your 100 square to try out different squares.*

Children can use PCM 3 and write on it if they find that helpful. Ask them to think about how they will record their results.

Teacher focus for activity

All abilities: If any children have difficulty with the addition involved, suggest that they use number lines to help them, as well as pencil-and-paper jottings. Encourage children to record their work carefully. They can draw arrows in their squares to remind them which numbers to total.

More able: Encourage children to work with larger numbers on the square and to move on quickly from a 4 square to a 9 square and then to a 16 square.

Average: Children may have more success if they make their squares using the numbers from 1 to 30, at least to begin with.

Less able: Children may be more comfortable working with smaller numbers from 1 to 20, making just a 4-number square.

As children work, ask questions, such as:

● *How did you work that out?*

● *If you chose that small square of numbers, would the opposite numbers total the same? Why is that, do you think?*

● *What if you chose a larger square? What do you think would happen then?*

● *How did you total those numbers? What strategies did you use?*

Optional adult input

Work with the Less able group. Children can all work to total the diagonal numbers in an agreed square. Encourage children to think about how they can record what they find out.

Plenary

1 Use a large, class 100 square. Invite individual children to draw around one of their 2 × 2 squares, draw in the arrows and give the totals, which should be the same. Repeat this for 3 × 3 squares, then for 4 × 4 squares.

   Ask:

   - *What do you notice about the totals each time?* (They are the same for each square.)

   - *Why do you think that is?*

   Invite children to speculate about this and praise them for their thoughts. Some may have noticed that if each pair of numbers is compared, there are always the same tens and units, but formed into different numbers. For example for the number pairs 15 and 37 and 17 and 35, each pair has a 10, a 30, a 7 and a 5, so that the same tens and units are being totalled.

2 Ask:

   - *Suppose we chose a 5 × 5 square. What do you think would happen then?*

   Draw around the following square:

3	4	5	6	7
13	14	15	16	17
23	24	25	26	27
33	34	35	36	37
43	44	45	46	47

   Ask children to total the diagonally opposite numbers in their heads: 3 + 47 = 50 and 7 + 43 = 50

   Invite a child to choose another 5 × 5 square, then a 6 × 6 one, and check again that the opposite diagonal numbers always total the same. Finally, total the opposite corners of the 100 square – that is, 1 and 100 and 10 and 91.

Ask for examples of how children recorded their results. Discuss how, where the addition sums have been written down, it is possible to see the relationship between the 2 pairs of numbers in each case.

Development

What could we try next with this problem? Suggestions could include trying 6 × 6, 7 × 7 . . . squares or trying diagonal opposites in rectangles. These ideas could form the basis for further investigation or for homework.

See **Useful mathematical information**, pages 84–85, for further information about the addition of diagonal numbers in a 100 square.

Solutions

The addition of opposite numbers in a square gives the same total. For example:

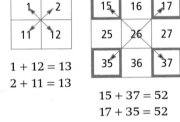

$1 + 12 = 13$
$2 + 11 = 13$

$15 + 37 = 52$
$17 + 35 = 52$

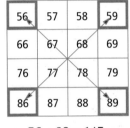

$56 + 89 = 145$
$59 + 86 = 145$

12 Solve it!

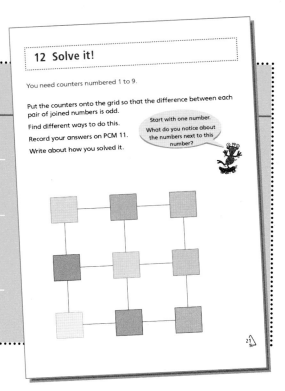

12 Solve it!

You need counters numbered 1 to 9.

Put the counters onto the grid so that the difference between each pair of joined numbers is odd.

Find different ways to do this.

Record your answers on PCM 11.

Write about how you solved it.

Start with one number. What do you notice about the numbers next to this number?

Minimum prior experience

finding differences; odd and even numbers

Resources

1–10 number lines (PCM 1), plain paper, counters with digits 1 to 9 for each pair, Textbook page 21, PCM 11

Key vocabulary

difference, odd, even, puzzle, calculate, method, right, correct, wrong

What's the problem

Each digit 1 to 9 must be placed on a grid so that the difference between any joined pair of numbers is odd.

Problem solving objectives

- Choose and use appropriate operations and efficient calculation strategies to solve problems.
- Solve mathematical problems or puzzles, recognise simple patterns and relationships, generalise and predict. Suggest extensions by asking 'What if . . . ?' or 'What could I try next?'
- Explain how a problem was solved orally and, where appropriate, in writing.

Differentiation

All children investigate the problem on Textbook page 21. The main differentiation is by outcome, although it may be helpful to give some children one or two starting numbers as a clue.

Introducing the problem

Provide each pair of children with counters numbered 1 to 9 and explain the problem: *Put the counters onto the grid on page 21 so that the difference between each pair of joined numbers is odd. Try and find different ways of doing this. Record your answers on the PCM and write some sentences to explain how you solved the problem.*

Teacher focus for activity

All abilities: Observe how children tackle the problem. Let children work for a few minutes, then make suggestions about ways of working.

More able: Check that children have a systematic way of working. Encourage them to explain how they have made odd differences. Ask: *What if I put this number down. Would the differences be odd or even? What else could you try?*

Average and Less able: When children are putting counters down randomly, say:

- *Which pairs of numbers will have odd differences? Try putting some of these pairs onto the grid. What else will fit in now?*
- *What if I put the 6 and the 9 next to each other? Is the difference odd or even? What should I try next?*

Less able: It may be helpful to suggest a starting point, e.g. *Try putting 5 in the centre square. What numbers could you put in the squares joined to it?*

Check that children understand that the differences must be odd for all pairs of joined numbers, so that for each number placed on the grid they will need to check two or more totals. Children may wish to use number lines to help them find differences, if they cannot work these out mentally.

Optional adult input

Work with the Less able group. Ask: *What if we place the 5 in the centre?* Work through the possibilities together, putting in the numbers next to the 5 first. Then investigate what happens if you start with an even number in the centre.

Plenary

1   Draw a large outline of the problem grid on the board. Invite children from each group to fill in a solution to the problem. Ask:

- *Why is there always an even number next to an odd number?*

- *How do we make an even difference? How do we make an odd difference?*

- *What do you notice about the position of the odd and even numbers?*

Invite various children to read what they have written about how they solved the puzzle. Ask them to explain the strategies that they chose and why these worked.

Strategies could include:

- Starting with 1 and placing the digits in order onto the grid. This would give an odd difference between each pair of numbers.

- Choosing any number, noting whether it is odd or even, and then putting a number to make an odd difference next to it. (Some children may realise that it is not necessary to work out the difference, as long as an odd number is always placed next to an even one.)

2   Discuss how making a plan and trying it out helps. Ask which children kept notes on what they had tried. Suggest to children that when trying out activities like this it is helpful to keep a note of what worked and of what did not work, so that there is a reminder of what has been tried. Explain that looking at the recording of what did not work can help to suggest what else to try.

3   Discuss the patterns that emerge through this activity: that an odd and even pairing is needed each time to produce an odd difference. See **Useful mathematical information**, page 85, for further information.

Development

Is it possible to solve the puzzle so that all of the differences are even?

Solutions

The difference between 2 odd numbers or 2 even numbers is always even, e.g. $9 - 7 = 2$ and $8 - 4 = 4$

The difference between an odd number and an even number is always odd, e.g. $8 - 5 = 3$ and $7 - 4 = 3$

It is not possible to solve the puzzle with all even differences, because if the starting number on the grid is odd, then all the other numbers would need to be odd; if the starting number on the grid were even, then all of the other numbers must be even. There are both odd and even numbers to be used on the grid.

The following are possible solutions. Note how, in each solution, if a number is odd, then the adjoining numbers are even, and if a number is even, the adjoining numbers are odd.

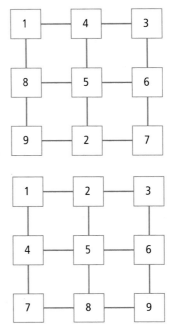

In any solution, the numbers in the centre and corner squares must be odd, because with even numbers at the 4 corners, an even number is also needed as a centre number. This is not possible as there are 5 odd and 4 even numbers within the numbers 1 to 9.

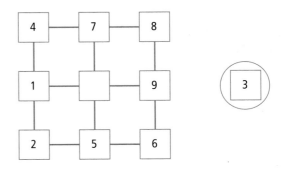

45

13 Equal totals

Minimum prior experience

adding more than 2 numbers

Resources

small counters with digits 3–6 (1–4 for Less able) (4 of each digit for each pair or child), Textbook page 22, 1–30 number lines, PCM 12

Key vocabulary

add, plus, total, puzzle, calculate, method, jotting, correct, row, column, diagonal, solution

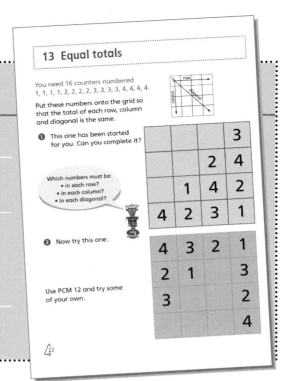

What's the problem?

Using just the numbers 3, 4, 5 and 6, children find ways of making each row, diagonal and column in a 4 × 4 square have the same total.

Problem solving objectives

- Choose and use appropriate operations and efficient calculation strategies to solve problems.
- Solve mathematical problems or puzzles, recognise simple patterns and relationships, generalise and predict. Suggest extensions by asking 'What if . . . ?' or 'What could I try next?'
- Explain how a problem was solved orally.

Differentiation

More able and Average: PCM 12.

Less able: Textbook page 22 gives a starting point for the activity. Children use PCM 12 for recording.

Introducing the problem

Explain the puzzle to children: *Use just the numbers 3, 4, 5 and 6. Put the numbers onto the grid so that each row, column and diagonal adds up to the same total. Each number can only be used once in any row or column.*

On the board, draw a simple diagram to help children to understand the terms row, column and diagonal.

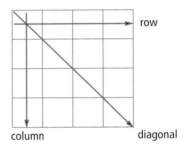

Ask children to talk through how they will start the problem with their partner. Remind them that you are interested in how they find their solution. Encourage them to keep a written record of what they try.

Teacher focus for activity

All abilities: Children will find it helpful to use PCM 12, which contains grids that they can use for recording their work.

More able: As children work, encourage them to find different solutions to the puzzle. Ask:

- *Is this the only solution?*
- *How else could you solve it?*
- *Will the answer always be the same? Why is that?*

Average: Suggest to children that they record their attempts at the puzzle, even if these are not correct. Ask:

- *Why do you think there are four 3s, four 4s, four 5s and four 6s?*

Less able: Textbook page 22 provides the same activity adapted for the less able, using numbers 1 to 4. Children complete examples before trying the open-ended activity.

As children work, ask questions, such as:

- *How could you make all the totals the same?* (For example, use 3, 4, 5 and 6 in each row, column and diagonal.)
- *What is the total here? And here? Are these the same? How could we make them the same?*

Optional adult input

Work with the Less able group, working together to explore different solutions.

Plenary

1 Draw a large 4 × 4 grid on the board and invite the Less able group to share their solutions and explain how they solved the problem.

   Invite children from the other groups to write up their solutions.

   - *What is the total in each column?*
   - *How do you know that the total must be 18?* (Because 3 + 4 + 5 + 6 = 18, and each row and column must contain each number.)
   - *How many different ways are there of making 18 using these numbers?* (3 + 4 + 5 + 6, 4 + 4 + 4 + 6, 3 + 3 + 6 + 6 and 5 + 5 + 5 + 3)

2 When there are several solutions on the board, look at the patterns that the solutions make.

   Ask:

   - *Do all of the diagonals have each of 3, 4, 5 and 6?*
   - *Why do you think that is?*

   See **Useful mathematical information**, page 85, for further discussion about using each of 3, 4, 5 and 6 in each row, column and diagonal.

   Ask:

   - *How did you start working at the problem?*
   - *Why did you start there?*
   - *Who looked for patterns?*
   - *What patterns did you find?*

3 Discuss how children recorded their solutions. Encourage children to discuss how to record what they have tried, so that they can learn from what they have found out. Some children may have written out each attempt that they made. Others may have tried to place the numbers randomly at first and then realised that one way of solving the

problem is to ensure that there is one each of 3, 4, 5 and 6 in each row. Ask children to explain how they ensured that the columns and diagonals also totalled 18.

Development

Encourage children to suggest how the problem could be extended. Suggestions might include:

- *What if we tried another 4 consecutive numbers?*
- *What if we tried just 3 numbers and a 3 × 3 grid?*
- *What if the numbers went up in 2s each time, such as 2, 4, 6 and 8 or 1, 3, 5 and 7?*

Solutions

Some possible solutions to the general problem are:

4	6	3	5
3	5	4	6
5	3	6	4
6	4	5	3

6	4	5	3
5	3	6	4
4	6	3	5
3	5	4	6

3	5	4	6
4	6	3	5
5	3	6	4
6	4	5	3

4	5	6	3
6	4	4	4
3	6	4	5
5	3	4	6

6	5	4	3
4	3	6	5
5	6	3	4
3	4	5	6

Solution to Textbook page 22: Using 1, 2, 3 and 4, the rows, columns and diagonals should total 10.

1

2	4	1	3
1	3	2	4
3	1	4	2
4	2	3	1

2

4	3	2	1
2	1	4	3
3	4	1	2
1	2	3	4

14 Make fifteen

Minimum prior experience

rapid recall of pairs of numbers to 20

Resources

teaching set of digit cards 1 to 9, paper for recording, coin, Textbook page 23, 0–20 number lines (PCM 1), PCM 4 Digit cards

Key vocabulary

add, more, plus, make, sum, total, altogether, puzzle, calculate, mental calculation, method

What's the problem?

Children find trios of cards that total 15.

Problem solving objectives

- Choose and use appropriate operations and efficient calculation strategies to solve problems.
- Solve mathematical problems or puzzles, recognise simple patterns and relationships, generalise and predict. Suggest extensions by asking 'What if . . . ?' or 'What could I try next?'
- Explain how a problem was solved orally.

Differentiation

The activity on Textbook page 23 is differentiated by the resources used to aid calculation.

Introducing the problem

Ask pairs of children to place their digit cards in order in a line. Explain that they take turns to take a card and place their card in front of them, face up, so that their partner can always see their cards. Tell children that they continue to take cards until one of them can choose 3 of the cards in front of them to give a total of 15.

Children play the game a number of times. Ask them to try to find a way of winning the game.

Teacher focus for activity

All abilities: Children may find it useful to have paper and pencil beside them to make jottings about number combinations as they play the game. Encourage them to write a number sentence for each total of 15 that they make.

More able: Ask questions such as: *What do you notice about the way you made 15? Is there another way to do this? How many different ways can you find?*

Average and Less able: Encourage children to play the game a few times, using the number line to help check totals. Then challenge them to find a winning strategy.

As children work, ask questions such as:
- *Who won?*
- *Who started first?*
- *Does it make a difference if you started first?*
- *How did you make 15?*
- *How else could you make 15?*

Optional adult input

Work with the Less able group. With children, develop a strategy for making 15, e.g. take the '5' and make 10 with two more cards or take the '4' and make 11 with the next two. *Which is the best card to take first?*

Plenary

1 Invite children to give some of their ideas about how to win the game. Their suggestions may include:

   ● always go first;

   ● decide how to make 15, then try to take those cards;

   ● take cards that total 10, then check each time to see if it is possible to use the 10 to make 15;

   ● watch what your partner takes, and make sure you take the card that they need.

   Discuss each of these suggestions. For example, going first does not ensure that you will win. Deciding on one way to make 15 gives your partner the opportunity to take the card that you need.

2 Looking for ways of making 10 is a good strategy. Ask:

   ● *How does taking cards that total 10 help you?*

   Children may realise that there are more ways to make 10 than to make other numbers, and the player who takes the 5 card is most likely to win, if they have adopted the 'make 10' strategy.

   On the board, write pairs of numbers that total 10:

1 + 9	6 + 4
2 + 8	7 + 3
3 + 7	8 + 2
4 + 6	9 + 1
5 + 5	

   Ask:

   ● *What do you notice about these pairs?*

   Children should notice that each pair is repeated: for example, that 1 + 9 is the same as 9 + 1, and that 5 + 5 is impossible because there is only one 5 card available. See **Useful mathematical information**, page 85, for more discussion about totalling 10.

3 Play the game again, this time dividing the class into 2 teams, with a leader for each group. Toss a coin to agree which team begins. If the team that begins takes 5 as their first card, then that team should win. Play again, and let the other team go first this time.

   Some children may have won without using this strategy. Ask children to explain what they did, and ask if the class thinks that that strategy would work every time. Discuss how, sometimes, you can just be lucky and win.

Development

Suggest to children that they play this game at home with their family and see if they can win every time. Suggest that they explain how to win when the family has had enough of losing! This will help children to use mathematical language at home and will also give further practice in rapid recall of number bonds to 10.

Solutions

Ways of totalling 15

Making 10 and adding 5:
1, 9, 5
2, 8, 5
3, 7, 5
4, 6, 5

Other ways:
9, 2, 4
8, 3, 4
8, 1, 6
7, 6, 2

15 Counter shapes

Minimum prior experience

multiplication

Resources

counters, squared paper, dotty paper, Textbook pages 24–25

Key vocabulary

count, multiply, array, row, column, left over, rectangle, square

15 Counter shapes

You need some counters.

❶ Count out 12 counters.

Put some of your counters onto the grid to make a rectangle.

Which numbers of counters will make rectangles?

❷ Count out 20 counters.

Put 10 of your counters onto the grid to make a rectangle.

Try making rectangles with other numbers of counters.

Which numbers will make more than one rectangle?

Investigate numbers bigger than 10.

❸ Count out 30 counters.

Put 20 of your counters onto the grid to make a rectangle. Record your array.

Try making rectangles with other numbers of counters.

Which numbers make more than one rectangle?

Investigate numbers larger than 20.

Try a small number of counters first. Now try adding one more counter, and one more again.

24

What's the problem?

Exploring multiplications with the same totals.

Problem solving objectives

- Choose and use appropriate operations and efficient calculation strategies to solve problems.
- Solve mathematical problems or puzzles, recognise simple patterns and relationships, generalise and predict. Suggest extensions by asking 'What if . . . ?' or 'What could I try next?'
- Explain how a problem was solved orally.

Differentiation

More able: Textbook pages 24–25, problem 3. Use 30 counters.

Average: Textbook pages 24–25, problem 2. Use 20 counters.

Less able: Textbook pages 24–25, problem 1. Use 12 counters.

Introducing the problem

Draw a 4×2 grid. *This grid can be called an array, because the squares are arranged in rows and columns.* Remind children that the array can be used to show the multiplication 4×2. Draw a 2×4 grid and discuss how the answers to 4×2 and 2×4 are the same. Explain the problem: *Take a small number of counters. Try to make a rectangle with them on the square grid in your book. Can you make a rectangle with the counters? Now think of a way of recording what you have done.*

I want you to try other numbers of counters.

Teacher focus for activity

All abilities: Children may need prompts about how to record. They could draw the arrays on dotty or squared paper. Encourage them to make tables of their results, so that they can search for patterns.

More able: Children should begin to identify arrays for times tables other than 2, 5 and 10.

Average: Children should realise that, for example, 4×5 gives the same answer as 5×4.

Less able: Children should be able to link multiplication totals up to 12 with the 2 times table.

Some questions to ask children as they work include:

- *What do you know about the number . . . ?*
- *How did you find that out?*
- *Which of these numbers are in the 2/3/4 . . . times table? How do you know that?*
- *Can you make a different rectangle with these counters?*
- *What if I added one more counter to these – could you make a different rectangle? What would it be?*

Optional adult input

Work with the More able group. Encourage children to explore each number in turn to find out what quantities will make 2 or more different rectangles.

50

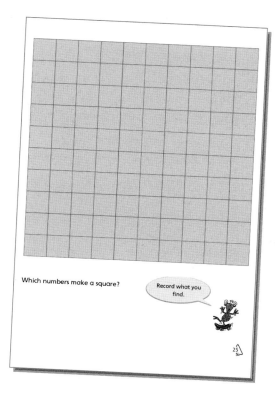

Which numbers make a square?

Record what you find.

Plenary

1   Ask the Less able group for some rectangle numbers. Write these on the board, in order.

- *What sort of rectangle can we make with 1/2/3 . . . ?*

- *What is the first number with which we can make a rectangle with more than one row?* (4)

- *What is the next rectangle we can make with more than one row?* (6)

- *What rectangles can we make with 12 counters?* (2 × 6, 6 × 2, 3 × 4 and 4 × 3)

2   Discuss whether a 2 × 6 rectangle is the same as a 6 × 2 rectangle. If necessary, draw a 2 × 6 rectangle and a 6 × 2 rectangle on a sheet of paper and turn the paper sideways so that children can compare the rectangles. Discuss how they are the same.

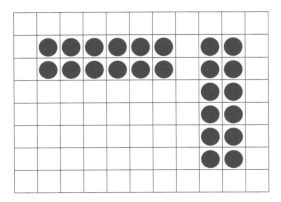

- *Which other numbers made lots of different rectangles?* (see **Solutions**)

- *What do you notice about the numbers 12, 18 and 30?* (Multiples of 6, which is a multiple of 2 and 3)

- *What is special about 20 and 30?* (Multiples of 10)

- *What might the next number be with lots of rectangles? Why do you think that?*

- *Think about the number 31. Do you think that you can make a rectangle with 2 rows for this number? Why do you think that? What about 3 rows?*

- *What can you say about numbers that make rectangles with 2 rows?* (e.g. in the 2 times table) *What about 3-row/4-row . . . numbers?*

3   Ask the More able group about numbers that make squares. They should have found 25 and may be able to predict others, e.g. 2 × 2, 3 × 3 and 4 × 4. Children can make these squares on their grids with the counters. See **Useful mathematical information**, pages 85–86, for discussion about rectangular and square numbers.

4   Discuss how children recorded their work: who was systematic, starting with the least amount of counters and moving on one counter each time. Some may have drawn rectangles, others may have made a table, others may have done both.

Solutions

Numbers 1, 2, 3, 5, 7, 11, 13, 17, 19, 23 and 29 will only produce a 1-row rectangle. Two or more row rectangles can be produced as follows:

Total	Rectangles
4	2 × 2
6	3 × 2, 2 × 3
8	4 × 2, 2 × 4
9	3 × 3
10	5 × 2, 2 × 5
12	6 × 2, 4 × 3, 3 × 4, 2 × 6
14	7 × 2, 2 × 7
15	5 × 3, 3 × 5
16	8 × 2, 4 × 4, 2 × 8
18	9 × 2, 6 × 3, 3 × 6, 2 × 9
20	10 × 2, 5 × 4, 4 × 5, 2 × 10
21	7 × 3, 3 × 7
22	11 × 2 (2 × 11)
24	12 × 2, 8 × 3, 6 × 4, 4 × 6, 3 × 8 (2 × 12)
25	5 × 5
26	13 × 2 (2 × 13)
27	9 × 3, 3 × 9
28	14 × 2, 7 × 4, 4 × 7 (2 × 14)
30	15 × 2, 10 × 3, 6 × 5, 5 × 6, 3 × 10 (2 × 15)

16 Two-dice totals

Minimum prior experience

rapid recall of addition number bonds to 12

Resources

paper for recording, counters, dice, Textbook page 26, 1–15 number line (PCM 1)

Key vocabulary

add, total, altogether, pattern, calculate, method, jotting, answer, number sentence

16 Two-dice totals

Investigate this puzzle with your partner.

Take turns to roll 2 dice.

Add the dice scores to find the total.

Cover the total on the grid.
Can you cover all of the numbers?

Can you cover some numbers more than once?

Which numbers can you make in different ways?
Which numbers can be made in only one way?

Which numbers can be made in different ways with 2 dice?

1	2	3
4	5	6
7	8	9
10	11	12

26

What's the problem?

This problem involves finding number pairs that make totals up to 12. Children use 2 dice and try to cover all of the numbers on the grid. As they play the game again, they will find that some different combinations of dice scores produce the same totals.

Problem solving objectives

- Solve mathematical problems or puzzles, recognise simple patterns and relationships, generalise and predict.
- Explain how a problem was solved orally.

Differentiation

All children play the game on Textbook page 26. Differentiation is by outcome and resources used.

Introducing the problem

Explain how to play the game: *Take turns to roll the 2 dice. Work out the total of the dice scores. Cover the total on the grid. The purpose is to investigate different ways of making the numbers using 2 dice. Some numbers can be covered more than once.*

Explain to children that you are interested in how they solve the problem and how they record what they do. Ask them to start the investigation immediately.

Teacher focus for activity

All abilities: Ask questions such as: *What can you tell me about the totals you have made? Tell me what you have noticed so far.*

More able: Children should know their number bonds to 12, so that the arithmetic should be straightforward for them. Now encourage them to investigate each number on the grid, to find different ways of making it from the total of 2 dice scores.

Average: Check that children can work out the scores mentally. When they have played the game once, ask them to find different ways of making each score. Ask: *How could you record what you find out?*

Less able: If children find it difficult to total the dice scores, suggest that they use number lines to help them. Encourage them to find different ways of making the totals 7, 8 and 9, using the dice numbers each time. They may work randomly at this, spotting number pairs that they know or can work out easily. Encourage them to start with one number and find as many addition pairs as they can for that number.

If children need extra help, suggest that they use 2 dice to make the score they are investigating.

Optional adult input

Work with the Average group. Encourage children to work systematically, starting from making the lowest possible total and moving up to the highest.

Plenary

1 Discuss what children found out about the numbers. Ask:

- *Can we make all of the totals from 1 to 12 with the 2 dice?*
- *Which number can we not make? (1)*
- *Why is that?*

Discuss how 1 cannot be made, because the lowest possible score with 2 dice is 2, that is, 1 + 1.

2 Invite individuals from each group to give their findings. These can be written on the board, making a simple table of results that shows the different combinations for each number.

```
2  1 + 1
3  1 + 2   2 + 1
4  1 + 3   2 + 2   3 + 1
```

Continue until all of the results are written up. If children have not found all of them, ask 2 children to each hold a large dice, and ask the others to think about different scores that could be made. Ask: *How else could we make 8?*

3 When the scores are completed, invite children to think about their results. Ask:

- *To make 7, should we record 3 + 4 as well as 4 + 3?*

Children may realise that it is possible to make both of these scores because they represent the scores on 2 different throws, i.e. 3 + 4 and 4 + 3.

Ask questions such as:

- *Which total can be made in the most ways?*
- *Which totals have the least number of ways of being made?*
- *If you play a game with 2 dice, which score is most likely to be made?*

Ask children to talk about how they recorded their work. Invite them to decide which were the better ways of recording and why.

Solutions

The dice scores can be made in the following ways:

Number	Scores					
1	No solution possible					
2	1 + 1					
3	1 + 2	2 + 1				
4	1 + 3	2 + 2	3 + 1			
5	1 + 4	2 + 3	3 + 2	4 + 1		
6	1 + 5	2 + 4	3 + 3	4 + 2	5 + 1	
7	1 + 6	2 + 5	3 + 4	4 + 3	5 + 2	6 + 1
8	2 + 6	3 + 5	4 + 4	5 + 3	6 + 2	
9	3 + 6	4 + 5	5 + 4	6 + 3		
10	4 + 6	5 + 5	6 + 4			
11	5 + 6	6 + 5				
12	6 + 6					

See **Useful mathematical information**, page 86, for a discussion about probability.

17 Animal quackers

17 Animal quackers

The farmer has some cows and some ducks in a field.
He counts their legs. There are 32 legs altogether.
How many cows and how many ducks are there?
Find different answers.

Stuck?
What if there were just 8 legs? Or 12?

Try different numbers of legs.
Suppose there were 10 legs, what then?
What patterns can you see in your answers?

Minimum prior experience

counting in 2s and 4s

Resources

interlocking cubes, toy cows and ducks, Textbook page 27,
0–50 number line (PCM 1), PCM 3 Hundred square

Key vocabulary

altogether, lots of, groups of, times, multiply, multiplied by, double,
group in 2s/4s, number sentence

What's the problem

Children find different ways of combining multiples of 2 and 4 to make 32.

Problem solving objectives

- Choose and use appropriate operations and efficient calculation strategies to solve problems.
- Solve mathematical problems or puzzles, recognise simple patterns and relationships, generalise and predict.
- Explain how a problem was solved orally and, where appropriate, in writing.

Differentiation

All children work on the problem on Textbook page 27. Differentiation is by outcome and resources, and by a suggestion that children use smaller starting numbers if appropriate.

Introducing the problem

Explain the problem to the children: *The farmer has some cows and ducks in a field. He counts all the legs and finds that there are 32 legs altogether. How many cows and how many ducks might there be?* Ask children to think about how they could begin to tackle the problem.

Remind them that they can choose their own method of recording what they have done and that you will be interested in how they tackle the problem. Also, say that you would like a number of different solutions.

Teacher focus for activity

All abilities: Encourage children to think about the possible combinations of animals, including having all cows and all ducks. Children may need some prompts about how to record the problem. Methods can include writing lists and tables, number sentences, drawing pictures then writing number sentences, drawing the legs of the animals . . .

Some questions to ask, as children work, include:

- *What happens if you start with only ducks in the field? How many ducks would there be?*
- *What happens if you add 1 cow?* (Need to lose 2 ducks, because 2 ducks or 1 cow have 4 legs.)
- *How did you find that solution?*
- *Why did you decide that you needed to add/multiply/double those numbers?*
- *From your results, can you work out another solution? How could you do that?*

More able: Children may begin to know their 4 times table, and through doubling their 2 facts will find facts for 4s. Encourage them to begin to use 4 times table facts.

Average: Children should make a link between the 2 times table and doubles for solving this problem. If children are having difficulty with larger numbers, suggest they try 12 legs.

Less able: Children may need to use apparatus to model the possible scenarios. If they find the numbers too large to manage, ask them to try the problem for 8 legs.

Optional adult input

Work with the Less able group. Children may need to see the problem visually; if so, they could model each animal with toy animals or interlocking cubes – 4 for a cow and 2 for a duck.

Plenary

1 Ask children from each ability group to explain how they solved the problem and check that the others understood what was done. It may help others to follow if children draw or write on the board. Discuss each method used, beginning with the simplest, such as making towers of cubes and counting them all. Ask children what they noticed about the number of legs that a cow has and the number that a duck has: a cow has twice as many as a duck. Encourage children to talk about how they used this fact. They may have used doubles, for example.

2 For each solution given verbally, ask: *How can we write that as a number sentence?* Encourage individuals to write number sentences on the flipchart and to use symbols correctly. For example, for 7 cows and 2 ducks write: '7 lots of 4 add 2 lots of 2' and ask: *How can we work out 7 lots of 4?* Give praise where children suggest such measures as 7×2 and double the answer. This sentence can then be rewritten as $7 \times 4 + 2 \times 2$.

3 Encourage children to look at the pattern that writing the results in a list will make (see **Solutions**). Ask: *What if there were just 12 legs? How could we write the solutions in a table?*

For 12 legs		
Cows	Ducks	Number sentences
0	6	0 x 4 + 6 x 2
1	4	1 x 4 + 4 x 2
2	2	2 x 4 + 2 x 2
3	0	3 x 4 + 0 x 2

Ask children to explain the pattern that they see. They may describe how the cows go 'up in 1s' and the ducks go 'down in 2s'. Rewrite the table, this time starting with zero ducks, then 1 duck, and ask: *Does this work? Why can't there be just 1 duck?* (There would be 10 legs left, which would give 2 cows, and legs left over.) See **Useful mathematical information**, page 86, for a discussion about combinations of multiples of 2 and 4.

When children have explored the different solutions, ask: *How could we change this problem so that we can have an odd number of ducks? What could we try next?*

Development

Extend the problem to 40 legs.

Solutions

The total number of legs, 32, is divisible both by 2 and by 4. The solutions can be summarised in a table:

Cows	Ducks
0	16
1	14
2	12
3	10
4	8
5	6
6	4
7	2
8	0

It is not possible to have an odd number of ducks, because there would be a spare set of 2 legs left over.

In order to produce an odd number of ducks, the total number of legs must be divisible by 2, but not by 4. So, for 10 legs:

Cows	Ducks
0	5
1	3
2	1

In this problem, it is not possible to have a solution with no ducks.

18 Digits

Minimum prior experience

recognising multiples of 10

Resources

plain paper, class register, Textbook page 28, 0–50 number line (PCM 1), PCM 3 Hundred square

Key vocabulary

count, count in . . ., multiples, guess, how many, estimate, nearly,

18 Digits

Look at this picture of Tom.

How many fingers does Tom have?

How many toes?

How many fingers and toes altogether?

Now look at this picture of Tom and Holly.

How many fingers do they have?

How many toes?

How many fingers and toes altogether?

What if there were 3 children?

How many fingers?

How many toes?

How many fingers and toes altogether?

Now try for 4, 5, 6 . . . children.

What pattern can you see?

Write about it.

28

What's the problem?

The problem involves finding multiples of 10 and 20.

Problem solving objectives

- Choose and use appropriate operations and efficient calculation strategies to solve problems.
- Solve mathematical problems or puzzles, recognise simple patterns and relationships, generalise and predict. Suggest extensions by asking 'What if . . . ?' or 'What could I try next?'
- Explain how a problem was solved orally and, where appropriate, in writing.

Differentiation

More able and Average: Work on the problem described below – differentiation is by outcome and by resources used or clues given.

Less able: Textbook page 28.

Introducing the problem

Say the problem: *Do you know what your digits are (apart from numbers 0 to 9)? Yes, they are fingers, thumbs and toes. Can you work out how many digits there are in the classroom? How many do you think there might be?* Ask children to think about how they could begin to tackle the problem. Tell them that they can choose their own method of recording and that you will be interested in the different ways that they use to tackle the problem.

Ask children to work on the problem straight away.

Teacher focus for activity

All abilities: To solve the problem, children need to find a way of finding multiples of 20. Discuss how to generate these multiples. Suggestions may include doubling multiples of 10.

More able: The children should make the link between the 10 times table and producing multiples of 20. Encourage them to show on paper how they tackle the problem.

Average: Suggest that children try to find the answer for fewer children. Then they can devise a method for finding how many digits for larger and larger numbers of children.

Less able: Children start with a much simpler case, such as how many digits 2 children have, then 5, before extending to larger numbers of children.

As they work, ask questions such as:

- *How many fingers and toes do you have?*
- *So how many fingers and toes will 2 people have?*
- *How many digits do you think there are in the classroom today? How did you work that out?*

Optional adult input

Work with the Average group. Suggest that children work out how many fingers and toes 1, then 2, then 5, then 10 children have. Ask questions such as: *How many fingers and toes do you have? How many do 2/5/10 children have? How did you work that out? How could you work out how many for 20 children? And for the whole class?*

Plenary

1 Invite children to discuss how many digits they estimated and how they worked out this estimate. Ask:

- *How many fingers and toes will one person have?* (20)

- *So how many will 2 have?* (40) *How did you work that out?* (For example, doubles)

- *So how did you work out how many there were altogether in the class today?*

2 Invite children from different groups to give their solutions. Discuss each solution and how it was reached. Encourage children to look for patterns. On the board, write:

Number of children	Number of digits
1	20
2	40
3	60

Ask:

- *What patterns can you see?* (For example, the number of digits is 20 times the number of children.)

- *Can you work out how many digits there would be for 5 children? How did you do that?*

- *So how many digits will there be for 10 children?*

Encourage children to extend the pattern, in multiples of 10, to the nearest 10 for the class. For example, for 32 children, extend the pattern to 30. Then ask children how to work out how many digits there are for 32 children.

3 Other children may have used different methods. Ask them to explain to the others how they worked out their answers. Discuss the different methods used and encourage children to decide which one they prefer and to explain why. Some children may have drawn pictures to show how many digits. Others may have used 5 times table facts and doubling.

4 Some children may note the links between multiples of 5, 10 and 20. (See **Useful mathematical information**, page 87.)

Development

Ask: *How could we change this problem? What could we try next?* Some suggestions might include how many thumbs are there or how many fingers.

Solutions

Each child will have 2 thumbs, 8 fingers and 10 toes, which makes a total of 20 digits.

The following table shows how many digits for different sized groups.

Number of children	Number of digits
15	300
16	320
17	340
18	360
19	380
20	400
21	420
22	440
23	460
24	480
25	500
26	520
27	540
28	560
29	580
30	600
31	620
32	640
33	660
34	680
35	700
36	720

The number of digits can be expressed as the number of children multiplied by 20.

19 Pocket money

Minimum prior experience

coin recognition and calculating totals

Resources

coins, paper, Textbook page 29

Key vocabulary

investigate, money, coin, pence, penny, pound, £, total, amount

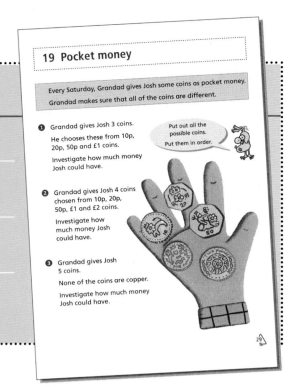

19 Pocket money

Every Saturday, Grandad gives Josh some coins as pocket money. Grandad makes sure that all of the coins are different.

❶ Grandad gives Josh 3 coins.
He chooses these from 10p, 20p, 50p and £1 coins.
Investigate how much money Josh could have.

Put out all the possible coins.
Put them in order.

❷ Grandad gives Josh 4 coins chosen from 10p, 20p, 50p, £1 and £2 coins.
Investigate how much money Josh could have.

❸ Grandad gives Josh 5 coins.
None of the coins are copper.
Investigate how much money Josh could have.

29

What's the problem?

An investigation into finding the range of possible values for a given number of coins.

Problem solving objectives

- Choose and use appropriate operations and efficient calculation strategies to solve problems.
- Use mental addition and subtraction to solve simple word problems involving money, using one or two steps.
- Recognise all coins and begin to use £ and p notation for money. Find totals.

Differentiation

More able: Textbook page 29, problem 3. Use 5 coins.

Average: Textbook page 29, problem 2. Use 4 coins.

Less able: Textbook page 29, problem 1. Use 3 coins.

Introducing the problem

Check that children recognise and remember all of the coins from 1p to £2, perhaps as an oral starter. Explain that the problem involves their understanding about coins and how to total them. Say: *On Saturday, Grandad gave Josh some coins as pocket money. Each coin was different. Your task is to investigate what different totals of money Josh might have.*

Explain that you are as interested in how children tackle the investigation as you are in their solutions. Ask them to record what they do. Each pair should then discuss how they will carry out the investigation.

Teacher focus for activity

All abilities: Encourage children to work systematically so that they do not miss possible solutions.

More able: Discuss with children how they could record their results. Encourage them to use tables or lists, and to work systematically, choosing 5 coins in an ordered way each time. Children may be able to work without the need for the coins in front of them, especially if they have built up a table in which to record their thinking. Check that children have included each of the coins from 5p to £2.

Average: Children will probably benefit from having coins available. If they do not collect these, and need help, suggest that they put one of each coin in order in front of them.

Less able: Decide whether to provide the full range of coins, or whether to remove the £1 and £2 coins. Encourage children to use the coins to help them. Check that they total the value of the coins, and not just the number of coins, for example, a 10p coin is seen as worth '10'.

Ask some questions as children work:

- *What is the least amount of money that Josh could have? And the most? How did you work that out?*
- *Tell me about the decisions you made for recording this.*

Optional adult input

Work with the Less able group, helping them to check the total of coins each time. Encourage them to be systematic.

Plenary

1 Ask children to explain what their problem was and how they solved it. Begin with problem 1. Ask:

- *You had 4 coins to choose from each time. So how many coins were left after you had chosen your 3 coins? (1)*
- *What was the smallest amount of money that Josh could have? (80p) How did you work that out?*
- *What was the most money that Josh could have? (£1.70) How did you work that out?*
- *How many possible solutions are there?*

2 Discuss how children recorded their results. Some of them may have drawn the coins and written their results. This could be shown, logically and systematically, like this:

Solution to problem 1

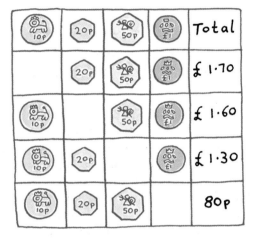

3 Consider problem 2 in the same way. Leave problem 1's results on the board. Invite children to give some of their solutions and write these on the board. Ask everyone to look at the solutions so far and to see if they can make some suggestions about other solutions. Invite the Average group to explain how they worked out the problem. Some children may have used the coins, and chosen 4 of the 5 each time; others may have made lists or written a simple table.

Solution to problem 2

10p	20p	50p	£1	£2	Total
	20p	50p	£1	£2	£3.70
10p		50p	£1	£2	£3.60
10p	20p		£1	£2	£3.30
10p	20p	50p		£2	£2.80
10p	20p	50p	£1		£1.80

4 Invite the More able group to show their results for problem 3, writing these on the board with the results for problems 1 and 2. Ask:

- *How did you solve the problem?*
- *How did you record your answers?*

Solution to problem 3

5p	10p	20p	50p	£1	£2	Total
	10p	20p	50p	£1	£2	£3.80
5p		20p	50p	£1	£2	£3.75
5p	10p		50p	£1	£2	£3.65
5p	10p	20p		£1	£2	£3.35
5p	10p	20p	50p		£2	£2.85
5p	10p	20p	50p	£1		£1.85

5 Where there has been a variety of ways of recording from the different groups of children, talk about which method children prefer and ask them to explain why. Discuss how a table can help you to see if any results have been missed.

6 Ask children to compare the 3 tables. Encourage them to see how many coins there were, how many were to be chosen each time and how many results there were.

Total number of coins	Number of coins chosen each time	Number of solutions
4	3	4
5	4	5
6	5	6

Ask children to comment on what they notice. See **Useful mathematical information**, page 87, for a discussion about probability.

Development

Ask: *What if some of the coins were the same? What would happen then?*

Solutions

See **Plenary**.

20 Leapfrog

Minimum prior experience

counting in 2s and 3s

Resources

counters, coloured pencils, paper, marker pens in various colours, large 1–100 number line, Textbook pages 30–31, PCM 13

Key vocabulary

count in 2s, count in 3s, multiple, every other, how many times?, pattern, method, jotting

20 Leapfrog

There are 2 frogs by the pond.
One is called Grunt and the other is called Croak.
In the pond, 30 stepping stones go from one side to the other.

❶ Grunt says 'I shall jump 2 stepping stones at a time'.
Croak says 'I shall jump 5 stepping stones at a time'.
Which stepping stones will they each land on?

❷ Grunt says 'I shall jump 2 stepping stones at a time'.
Croak says 'I shall jump 3 stepping stones at a time'.
Which stepping stones will they each land on?
Which stepping stones will not be visited?

What's the problem?

Children search for numbers with common multiples.

Problem solving objectives

- Solve mathematical problems or puzzles, recognise simple patterns and relationships.
- Explain how a problem was solved orally and, where appropriate, in writing.

Differentiation

More able: Textbook pages 30–31, problem 3.
Use multiples of 3 and 4.

Average: Textbook page 30, problem 2.
Use multiples of 2 and 3.

Less able: Textbook page 30, problem 1.
Use multiples of 2 and 5.

Introducing the problem

Describe the problem to the children: *By a pond sit 2 frogs, one called Grunt and the other called Croak. There are 30 stepping stones that go from one side of the pond to the other.* Ask children to find their activity in the Textbook. Check that they understand that each frog starts from the land, and that they understand how the frogs jump.

Remind children of the range of resources that you have put out so that they can discuss with their partner what they might need to use. Explain that you are as interested in how they tackle the problem as in the correct answer, and that they should record what they do.

Teacher focus for activity

All abilities: Ask children questions about how they will go about solving this problem, such as: *What do you need to solve the problem? How will you use that? Tell me what you will do next and why.* All children may find PCM 13 helpful as a means of recording the frogs' leaps.

More able: Children may need help with the counting patterns of 3s and 4s. If they find this difficult, suggest that they draw the leaps on PCM 13 with a different colour for each frog.

Average: Children should know counting in 2s, but may be less sure about counting in 3s. Suggest that they draw the leaps and write down the numbers that they land on. They may find a number line helpful.

Less able: Children may not be confident yet with counting in 2s and 5s. They can place counters on the number track on Textbook pages 30–31, a different colour for each frog.

❸ Grunt says 'I shall jump 3 stepping stones at a time'.
Croak says 'I shall jump 4 stepping stones at a time'.
Which stepping stones will they each land on?
Which stepping stones will not be visited?
Write some sentences to explain your results.

Use PCM 13.
Draw in Grunt's path across the stepping stones.
Now draw in Croak's path.

While children work, ask questions, such as:

- *Which numbers will Grunt land on? How do you know?*
- *And which numbers will Croak land on?*
- *Which numbers will they both land on? What can you tell me about those numbers?*

Optional adult input

Work with the More able group, checking that children recognise counting patterns in 3s and 4s.

Plenary

1   Begin with the Less able group. Draw a large version of PCM 13 and invite children to say which stepping stones Grunt, who leaps 2 each time, visits. Ask children to say the numbers aloud and mark them on the picture. Ask them to repeat this for Croak, who leaps 5 each time, marking these in a different colour. Ask:

- *Which stepping stones are not visited? Why is this?* (Encourage children to explain that these numbers do not appear when counting in 2s or 5s.)
- *What sort of numbers are these?* (odd numbers)
- *Does Grunt land on any odd numbers?* (no) *Which odd numbers does Croak land on?* (any ending in 5)
- *Which stepping stones are visited by both frogs?*

Discuss how these numbers are multiples of 10, and that, for example, $2 \times 5 = 10$ and $4 \times 5 = 20 \ldots$

2   Now ask the Average group to give their findings in the same way.

Discuss how the numbers that are visited this time are in both the counting in 2s and 3s patterns. Ask:

- *What do you notice about these numbers?*

Children should be aware that the numbers visited by both frogs are even. This is because the pattern generates the multiples of 6.

3   Finally, look at the More able group's patterns, which involve counting in 3s and 4s. Again, mark the stones visited on the board and invite children to say which stones are visited by both frogs. There are only 2: 12 and 24. Ask:

- *Which stone do you think both frogs will visit next?*

If children cannot work this out, ask them to count on with you in 3s, starting from 30, and mark the numbers on a large number line. Repeat this, counting in 4s: 20, 24, 28, . . . (See **Useful mathematical information**, page 87, for discussion of multiples of 2, 3, 4, 6 and 12.)

Ask:

- *What do you notice about the numbers that both frogs visit?*

Children should note that these are all even numbers. (They are also multiples of 12, but it is unlikely that children will understand this yet.)

Solutions

The pairs of frogs both land on common multiples:

1   2s and 5s: multiples of 10: 10, 20, 30 . . .
($2 \times 5 = 10$)

2   2s and 3s: multiples of 6: 6, 12, 18 . . .
($2 \times 3 = 6$)

3   3s and 4s: multiples of 12: 12, 24, 36 . . .
($3 \times 4 = 12$)

21 Make a shape

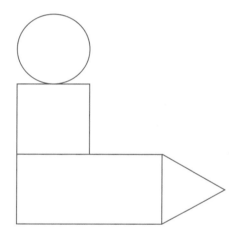

21 Make a shape

Make a screen between you and your partner.
One of you make a shape from the shape tiles.
Now describe the shape you have made to your partner.
Can your partner make the same shape?

These words may help you.

top   bottom   side
between   opposite
corner   left   next to
right   edge   beside
centre   below   above   under   middle
over   underneath

Listen carefully to
your partner.
Put each shape where you are told.
Do just one piece
at a time.

32

Minimum prior experience

naming 2-D shapes and exploring their properties

Resources

scissors, shape tiles of squares, rectangles, circles, triangles,
pentagons, hexagons and octagons (use PCM 14 and PCM 15 if
shape tiles are not available), overhead projector, large books, glue,
paper, Textbook page 32

Key vocabulary

position, above, below, top, bottom, between, left, right, next to,
middle, edge, circle, triangle, square, rectangle, pentagon,
hexagon, octagon

What's the problem?

This activity gives children the opportunity to listen
to and use the mathematical language of shape,
position and direction, and to give and follow
instructions carefully. For the activity to be completed
successfully, each child must concentrate on what
they say and what they hear.

Problem solving objectives

- Solve mathematical problems or puzzles, recognise
  simple patterns and relationships, generalise and
  predict. Suggest extensions by asking 'What if . . . ?'
  or 'What could I try next?'

- Explain how a problem was solved orally.

Differentiation

All abilities: Textbook page 32. Differentiate by the
range of shapes used with each group:

More able: Squares, rectangles, circles, triangles,
pentagons, hexagons and octagons.

Average: Squares, rectangles, circles, triangles and
pentagons.

Less able: Squares, rectangles, circles and triangles.

Introducing the problem

Provide children with 4 shape tiles: a square,
rectangle, circle and triangle. Model the activity so
that they understand what to do. Place a set of shapes
onto the overhead projector to make the design
shown here, but do not turn the light on.

Say the following slowly, pausing between each
sentence to give children time to carry out your
instructions: *Put the square down in front of you. Put the
circle at the top of the square, in the middle, so that it just
touches it. Now put the rectangle under the square so that
one long side of the rectangle is against the square, and the
left-hand sides of the square and rectangle line up to make a
straight line. At the right-hand side of the rectangle, place
the triangle so that one side of it is against the short side of
the rectangle, with the middles matching.*

When children have finished, switch on the overhead
projector's lamp so that they can compare what they
did with your design.

Explain that children should take it in turns to make
a design with their shapes and give instructions to
their partner to make the same shape. They can make
a screen by standing a large book, slightly open,
between them so that they cannot copy each other's
designs. Tell them that 5 minutes before the plenary
you will give them time to record their favourite
design.

Teacher focus for activity

All abilities: Check that children listen to each other carefully, and discourage peeping from around the screen. Listen to the children's descriptions of the position of the shapes and encourage them to use appropriate vocabulary.

More able: Suggest to children that they incorporate more than one square, rectangle . . . in order to build up more complex designs.

Average: Encourage children to make various designs from their shapes and to describe the position of the shapes as accurately as they can.

Less able: Check that children can follow directions that include 'left' and 'right'.

As children work, ask questions such as:
- *Where is that piece to go?*
- *What could you put here?*
- *How else could you describe the position of that shape?*

Optional adult input

Work with the Less able group, listening carefully to their descriptions. If children find this activity difficult, make a design, unseen by the children, and describe it for the group to make.

Plenary

1 Ask children to remain sitting at their tables, with some more shapes in front of them. Invite various children to describe their favourite design for the others to make. Children can check that they have made their design correctly by viewing the original.

2 Invite children to list the important vocabulary that they used. This can be written on the board. Words may include: left, right, between, alongside, next to . . . and so on. Some children may still find left and right confusing.

3 Ask:
- *What did you enjoy about this activity? Why was that?*
- *What did you find difficult? Why do you think that was?*
- *What does the person describing the position need to do so that you can copy their shape accurately?*
- *What have you learned from doing this activity?*
- *How could we change the activity?*

Success with this activity involves understanding about the properties of 2-D shapes and being able to use shape language appropriately and accurately. See also **Useful mathematical information**, pages 87–88.

Development

Children may like to try the same activity again and, as an extension, this time use 3-D shapes.

22 Shape pairs

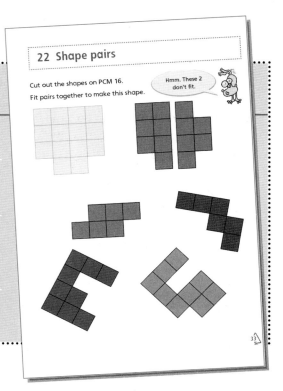

Minimum prior experience

fitting together shape tiles

Resources

scissors, glue, paper, mirrors, Blu-Tack, Textbook page 33, PCM 16, A3 enlargement of PCM 16 with the shapes cut out

Key vocabulary

line of symmetry, match, mirror line, reflection, puzzle

What's the problem?

The PCM contains 12 shapes to be cut out and paired to make the shape shown in the Textbook.

Problem solving objectives

- Solve mathematical problems or puzzles, recognise simple patterns and relationships. Suggest extensions by asking '*What if . . . ?*' and '*What could I try next?*'
- Explain how a problem was solved orally.

Differentiation

The activity on Textbook page 33 is for the whole class, with differentiation by outcome.

Introducing the problem

Ask children to begin by cutting out the shapes on their PCM. With one sheet between 2 children, this should not take very long. Demonstrate quick ways of doing this, e.g. cutting across whole rows first. Ask children to look at the shape on Textbook page 33. Explain that you would like them to find pairs of shapes that will combine to make the shape on the page.

Ask them to think about how they will record their work. They should begin the problem straight away.

Teacher focus for activity

All abilities: Observe children as they begin the task and check that everyone understands what they are doing.

More able: Encourage children to explain their results. They may notice that the whole shape is symmetrical. Encourage them to use a mirror to observe this by moving the mirror around on the shape to find the mirror line or line of symmetry. (See also **Useful mathematical information**, page 88, for more on symmetry.)

Average and Less able: If children find this activity difficult, encourage them to place one piece onto the outline in the Textbook and to try different pieces until they complete the shape.

Possible hints:

- *Try turning the pieces. Can you find one that fits now?*
- *What sort of shape do you need to finish this one? Describe it to me.*

Optional adult input

Work with the Less able group and encourage them to turn the pieces to find one that fits.

Plenary

1 Using the enlarged shape pieces, invite various children to show which shapes they have paired together to make the shape in the Textbook. As they make each shape, place these onto the board with Blu-Tack. Encourage children from each ability group to take part in this.

2 When all of the pairs have been made, ask questions such as:

- *How did you find out that these pieces fitted together to make the shape?*

- *What clues did you use to make the shapes?*

Take a pair of shapes and remove one of the pieces. Now point to the one that is left and ask:

- *What do you need to complete the shape? Describe the piece to me.*

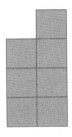 

Encourage children to describe accurately what is missing. If they find this difficult, place the shape that is on the board over the completed shape so that they can see what they need to describe. Repeat this for other shapes, until children are more confident with this.

3 Now ask children to look carefully at the whole shape and ask what they notice. Encourage More able children to discuss the mirror line (line of symmetry) and invite one of these children to show this to the others.

4 Provide mirrors for each pair of children and ask them to place their mirror along the mirror line of the shape and then to look in the mirror. Encourage them to describe what they can see.

Development

Children could make their own shape and pairs of pieces that fit onto it. The other children could use these in a subsequent lesson.

Solutions

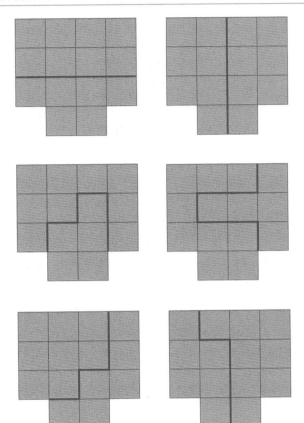

23 Cube shapes

Minimum prior experience

building shapes with interlocking cubes

Resources

interlocking cubes, squared paper, plain paper, Textbook page 34

Key vocabulary

cube, shape, pattern, flat, puzzle, what could we try next?, how did you work it out?

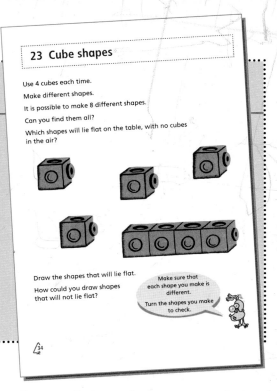

23 Cube shapes

Use 4 cubes each time.
Make different shapes.
It is possible to make 8 different shapes.
Can you find them all?
Which shapes will lie flat on the table, with no cubes in the air?

Draw the shapes that will lie flat.
How could you draw shapes that will not lie flat?

Make sure that each shape you make is different.
Turn the shapes you make to check.

What's the problem?

Children explore the different shapes that can be made with 4 cubes. It is similar to the well-known pentominoes investigation, but easier.

Problem solving objectives

- Solve mathematical problems or puzzles, recognise simple patterns and relationships, generalise and predict. Suggest extensions by asking 'What if . . . ?' or 'What could I try next?'
- Explain how a problem was solved orally.

Differentiation

The activity on Textbook page 34 is for the whole class, with differentiation by outcome.

Introducing the problem

Ask children to take 4 cubes each and put them together to make a shape. Compare the shapes that children have made. Ask: *Who has a shape that will lie flat on the table with no cubes sticking up in the air?* Explain that you would like children to make as many shapes as they can, each with 4 cubes, and then to sort them into 2 piles: those that will lie flat and those that will not.

Teacher focus for activity

All abilities: As children work, encourage them to check the shapes that they have already made so that they do not have 2 shapes the same. Encourage them to turn the shapes to check that each is unique.

More able: Encourage children to find all 8 shapes and to sort them as they finish each one into 'lies flat' and 'does not lie flat'. Ask: *How will you record what you have done?*

Average: Check that children understand the difference between shapes that lie flat and shapes that do not, by choosing one of each and asking children to explain which shape can be placed flat.

Less able: Encourage children to check each one of their shapes carefully to make sure that it is unique. Where they have 2 the same, ask them to compare them and to turn just one of the shapes until they can see that both are the same.

Ask questions, such as:

- *How many shapes have you made?*
- *How many shapes lie flat?*
- *Can you find any shapes your partner has made that are the same as one of yours?*

Optional adult input

Work with the Less able group, helping them to check that all their shapes are unique by turning them.

Plenary

1 Invite various children to show shapes that they have made. Where children offer duplicate shapes demonstrate this by turning one of the shapes until they are both in the same orientation. Line the shapes up so that children can see all that have been made.

Ask:

- *Which shapes will lie flat?*
- *How many shapes will lie flat?*

Explain that there are 8 shapes altogether and that 5 of these can lie flat.

Invite various children to show how they recorded their shapes on squared paper. Discuss which way of recording was most suitable. Discuss which was easier to use – squared or plain paper – and why that was. Talk about the different ways children used to draw the 3-D shapes.

2 Ask children to shut their eyes and this time to imagine 3 cubes that can be joined together to make a shape that will lie flat. Ask children to open their eyes and invite 2 of them to make what they imagined. There are 2 possible solutions to this:

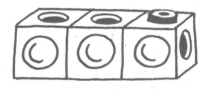

Ask:

- *When we use cubes, what do we mean by a 'flat' shape?* (A shape in which all the cubes touch the table.)
- *And what other sort of shapes can we make?*

3 Finally, put 2 of the same 'flat' shapes side by side, but in different orientations, and ask:

- *Are these different or the same shape?*
- *How can we tell?*

Invite a child to turn one of the shapes until both are in the same orientation.

See also **Useful mathematical information**, page 88, for more on making shapes with cubes.

Solutions

These are the possible shapes that can be made with 4 cubes.

There are 5 shapes that will lie flat (i.e. all cubes touching the table) and 3 that will not.

Shapes that will lie flat

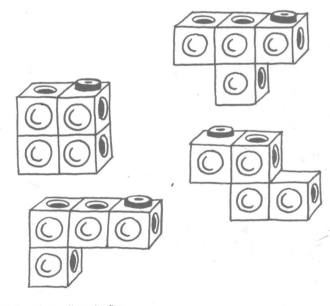

Shapes that will not lie flat

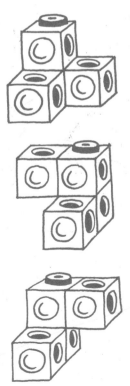

24 Four-sided shapes

Minimum prior experience

recognition of common 2-D shapes including square, rectangle, triangle and right angles

Resources

squared and plain paper, Textbook page 35, PCM 15 or 2-D shape tiles including square, rectangle and right-angled triangle (2 of each for each pair/child), (Polydron or Clixi could be used)

Key vocabulary

triangle, triangular, square, rectangle, rectangular, right-angled, quadrilateral, pentagon, hexagon, octagon, vertex, vertices, method, draw, sketch

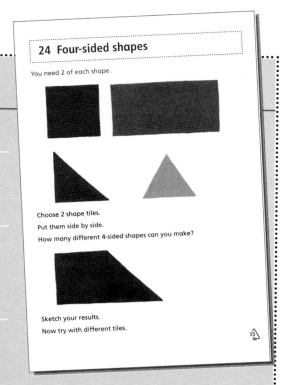

24 Four-sided shapes

You need 2 of each shape.

Choose 2 shape tiles.
Put them side by side.
How many different 4-sided shapes can you make?

Sketch your results.
Now try with different tiles.

35

What's the problem?

Using 2 tiles at a time, children investigate which 4-sided shapes they can make.

Problem solving objectives

● Solve mathematical problems or puzzles, recognise simple patterns and relationships, generalise and predict. Suggest extensions by asking 'What if . . .?' or 'What could I try next?'

● Explain how a problem was solved orally.

Differentiation

The activity on Textbook page 35 is for the whole class, with differentiation by outcome.

Introducing the problem

Ask children to look at the Textbook page and explain the problem. Say: *Look at the pictures of the square and the triangle. If they were pushed together, how many sides would the new shape have? Yes, 4.* Explain that children choose 2 tiles each time and investigate how many 4-sided shapes they can make with them.

Explain that you are interested in the choice of shapes that they make as well as the way in which they record the activity. Ask children to discuss how they will start the investigation and to begin at once.

Teacher focus for activity

All abilities: Encourage children to explore the shapes that they can make from 2 shape tiles. If children find this difficult, suggest that they try turning one tile over to see if it produces a different result. They will find it possible to make shapes other than 4-sided ones.

More able: Explain that 4-sided shapes are called quadrilaterals. Ask questions such as:

● *What shape have you made?*

● *Is it a quadrilateral? Does it have a name?* (For example, rectangle, diamond, kite.)

(See also **Useful mathematical information**, page 88, for possible quadrilaterals.)

Encourage children to sketch the shapes that they make, including those that do not have 4 sides.

Average and Less able: Check that children are clear about the types of shapes that are required. Ask them to name and describe some 4-sided shapes, such as square, rectangle, diamond, kite . . . Encourage children to sketch what they find. They may find using squared paper helps them to be more accurate in their drawings.

Optional adult input

Work with the Less able group. Discuss each shape that children make, counting sides and angles, and naming the shape by the number of its sides.

Plenary

1   Invite a pair of children to choose 2 shape tiles and to demonstrate the range of shapes that they could make with these tiles. Sketch each shape made on the board and ask children to name it. If necessary, explain that any shape with, say, 5 sides, is a pentagon, and that the sides and vertices do not all have to be the same size. For example, with a triangle and a square, it is possible to make a 'house' shape that has 5 sides and is called a pentagon.

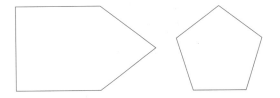

Continue to invite pairs of children to take pairs of shapes, until all of the 4-sided possibilities with 2 shapes have been found.

Ask questions as children give their solutions, such as:

- *How many sides does this shape have? And this?*
- *Can you make a 4-sided shape from these 2 shapes?*
- *Can you make another one from these 2 shapes?*
- *What other shapes can you make and what are their names?*

2   Invite pairs of children to show how they recorded their results. Discuss sketching as a means of recording and explain to children that it is quite acceptable to make a neat drawing of the shapes without using a ruler to draw the lines. Discuss how this is a quick way of recording, but that it should be done as neatly as possible.

Ask:

- *What sort of paper did you choose for your recording?*
- *Which sort do you think was best for this activity? Why?*

It is quite acceptable for children to choose to use squared paper if they believe that the lines will help them to produce a more accurate sketch.

3   Finally, ask children which shapes they made that did not have 4 sides, but that they thought were interesting shapes. They could demonstrate these by combining 2 shapes for the others to see.

Development

Ask: *What 4-sided shapes can you make using 3 tiles each time?*

Solutions

With the suggested tiles, there is a number of solutions.

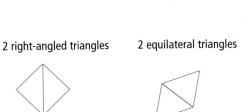

Square and rectangle

Equilateral and right-angled triangle

25 Four the same

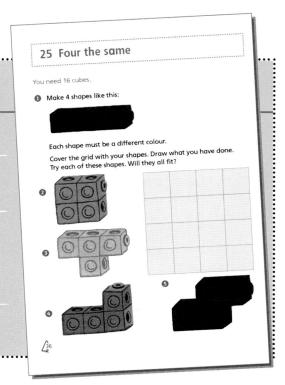

25 Four the same

You need 16 cubes.

1 Make 4 shapes like this:

Each shape must be a different colour.
Cover the grid with your shapes. Draw what you have done.
Try each of these shapes. Will they all fit?

2

3

5

4

36

Minimum prior experience

activity 23 Cube shapes

Resources

16 interlocking cubes for each pair of children (4 each of 4 different colours), squared paper, plain paper, coloured pencils, Blu-Tack, Textbook page 36

Key vocabulary

cube, shape, pattern, flat, puzzle, turn, what could we try next?, how did you work it out?

What's the problem?

Children explore fitting together 4 of the same shape in order to cover a square.

Problem solving objectives

- Solve mathematical problems or puzzles, recognise simple patterns and relationships, generalise and predict. Suggest extensions by asking 'What if . . . ?' or 'What could I try next?'
- Explain how a problem was solved orally.

Differentiation

All children use Textbook page 36: the Less able group may try only questions 1 to 3. Ask the More able group to start with question 5 and work backwards.

Introducing the problem

Ask children to look at Textbook page 36 and remind them of the cube shapes that they made for activity 23. *Can you remember the 5 shapes that would lie flat?* Explain the problem: *Make 4 of the shape that you will start with, making each one in a different colour. Now try to fit the 4 shapes onto the grid so that there are no spaces. When you have done this, find a way to record what you have done.*

Check that children understand what to do. Explain that you are as interested in how they solve the problem as in their solution. Ask them to begin the problem straight away.

Teacher focus for activity

All abilities: Check that children make 4 identical shapes each time.

More able: Children are expected to use each of the shapes in turn, so they will need to work quickly. They may find it helpful just to sketch their results on squared paper rather than to colour them in.

Average: Children may find it helpful just to sketch their results on squared paper rather than to colour them in.

Less able: Children may find it helpful to colour in the shapes on their squared paper so that they can see clearly how the shapes lie together.

As children work, ask questions such as:

- *How do these shapes fit together?*
- *Is there another way of doing this?*
- *Try turning the shape: will it fit now?*

Optional adult input

Work with the Average group and encourage them to explain how they are placing each shape. Discuss ways of recording the outcomes quickly.

Plenary

1 Invite the Less able group to give their solution to the first shape. Discuss where children have different solutions, as they will find that their solution is the same if they turn their paper. Repeat this with the next shape – the square. Now repeat this with the T shape.

Ask:

● *How did you work this out?*

● *How have you recorded this?*

Discuss the ways of recording, and praise children for their work.

2 Now consider the L shape with the Average group. Ask:

● *How did you fit these shapes together?*

Talk about how children turned some of the shapes to make them fit, but that these are still the same shapes. Use some cubes and demonstrate how this works, sticking the shapes onto the board with Blu-Tack.

3 Now consider the Z shape and invite the More able group to give their results. Ask:

● *Can you explain why this shape will not fit?*

● *How many Z shapes will fit onto the grid?*

● *How many squares are left uncovered?*

Discuss how the shape takes up 4 squares (the same number as the other shapes) and that 3 shapes will fit onto the grid. Explain that 4 squares are left uncovered, but not together to enable another Z shape to be placed on the grid.

Ask the More able group how they recorded their work. Discuss how, when time is short, it is possible to make a brief sketch of work to show what has been done.

Congratulate children on their achievements during this lesson.

Development

See **Useful mathematical information**, page 89. Try filling one of the 16-square grids pictured with a 4-cube shape.

Solutions

With

With

With

With

With

Note that it is not possible to fill a square with this shape.

26 Triangle trap

Minimum prior experience

recognition of triangles and properties of triangles, right angles

Resources

pin boards (5 × 5 to 10 × 10 pins), elastic bands, dotty paper, paper, Textbook page 37

Key vocabulary

shape, pattern, right-angled triangle, vertex, vertices, puzzle, method, jotting

26 Triangle trap

You need a pin board and some elastic bands.

Make some triangles on the pin board.

Find some triangles that will trap 1 pin.

Now find triangles that will trap 2 pins, 3 pins, 4 pins . . .

Can you find a triangle with no pins trapped?

Try different-shaped triangles.

What happens if you try a right-angled triangle?

37

What's the problem?

Children explore different shapes and sizes of triangles.

Problem solving objectives

- Solve mathematical problems or puzzles, recognise simple patterns and relationships, generalise and predict. Suggest extensions by asking 'What if . . . ?' or 'What could I try next?'
- Explain how a problem was solved orally and, where appropriate, in writing.

Differentiation

The activity on Textbook page 37 is for the whole class, with differentiation by outcome.

Introducing the problem

Say the problem: *You can make lots of different triangles on the pin boards. See if you can make a triangle that traps one pin without the elastic band touching it. Now can you trap 2 pins? Find different ways of doing this.*

Ask children to think about how they could begin to tackle the problem. Explain that you would like them to record what they do. Children should then tackle the problem immediately.

Teacher focus for activity

All abilities: Make sure that children understand what is meant by trapping a pin, demonstrating if necessary. Check how children are recording. They will probably draw their triangles on dotty paper.

More able: Encourage children to find several different examples for each number of pins trapped.

Average: Suggest to children that they try to find 2 examples of each trapping.

Less able: Suggest to children that they find a triangle that will trap one pin, then 2 pins, and so on.

As children work, ask questions about what they have found out, such as:

- *How many pins have you trapped?*
- *How many rows of pins are there in your triangle from top to bottom?*
- *What connection is there between the number of rows and the number of pins trapped?*
- *What if you made your triangle one row longer? How many pins do you think would be trapped then?*

Optional adult input

Work with the Less able group. At first, children may need to explore putting elastic bands onto the pin boards to make triangles. Make sure that the exploration stage does not last too long. Discuss with children how they will record their results. They may need reminding that dotty paper is available.

Plenary

1 Ask children to give some examples of triangles that trap just one pin. Make an isosceles triangle, with a base covering 3 pins and a height of 3 pins. This will trap one pin. Ask:

- *How many rows of pins does this triangle cover?*
- *If I stretch this triangle by one more row, how many pins will be trapped?*
- *And one more row? What about one more?*
- *Is there a link between the number of rows and the number of pins trapped for this triangle?*
- *If we made a triangle 10 rows long, how many pins would be trapped?*

Encourage children to see that there are 2 fewer trapped pins than the number of rows. Some children may have made this connection themselves.

2 Now repeat this with a right-angled triangle, starting with one that is 2 pins high and 3 pins along the base. As the pattern grows, ask:

- *Is this the same pattern as for the other triangles?*
- *What do you notice about the pattern?*
- *What if I made a triangle 13/16 . . . rows long?*

3 Ask children to describe the different types of triangle that they tried. Discuss which triangles have a right angle. See also **Useful mathematical information**, page 89, for further information about triangles.

4 Discuss how children recorded their work. When different recording methods were used, ask them to decide which was the most effective and why. Remind them that drawing the triangles was very useful as they had a record of what they did. Remind them, too, that making a table to show how many rows and how many trapped pins helps with spotting patterns.

5 Finally, ask which triangles trapped no pins.

Solutions

The base size of the triangles will alter the pattern of spots.

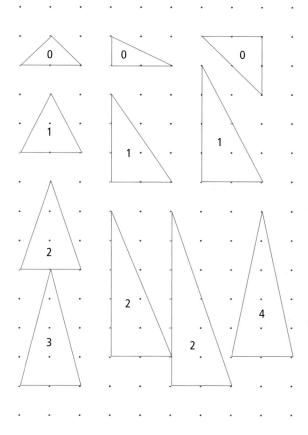

Isosceles triangles

Number of rows of pins	Number of pins trapped
2	0
3	1
4	2
5	3

Right-angled triangles

Number of rows of pins	Number of pins trapped
2	0
3	0
4	1
5	1
6	2
7	2
8	3
9	3
10	4
11	4
12	5
13	5

27 Favourite TV programmes

Minimum prior experience

know how many minutes in an hour; calculate times in quarter hours; read digital and analogue time

Resources

paper for recording, Textbook pages 38 and 39, PCM 17 (on card if possible), large teaching clock face

Key vocabulary

hour, minute, quarter, half, how long, takes longer, takes less time

What's the problem?

Children are asked to fill a videotape with programmes. Textbook page 39 gives a programme listing for a Saturday, with times to the quarter hour.

Problem solving objectives

- Choose and use appropriate operations and efficient calculation strategies to solve problems.
- Explain how a problem was solved orally and, where appropriate, in writing.
- Use mental addition and subtraction to solve simple word problems involving time, using one or two steps.

Differentiation

More able: Textbook pages 38–39, problem 3. 3-hour tape.

Average: Textbook pages 38–39, problem 2. 2-hour tape.

Less able: Textbook pages 38–39, problem 1. 1-hour tape.

Introducing the problem

Ask children:

- *When do you record your favourite programmes?*
- *Do you set the video machine at home?*
- *How do you know how much room there is on the tape?*

Explain that you would like children to use the TV guide on Textbook page 39 just as they might do at home. Check that all children understand how to read the guide in digital time. Discuss how the video at home usually needs an extra few minutes before and after the programme, but for today's lesson there is no need to include that.

Teacher focus for activity

All abilities: Check that children are clear about the total amount of time that they have to fill the tape and that they can convert from digital to analogue time.

More able: Encourage children to make jottings as they decide their programmes. They may find it helpful to record how long each programme lasts and how much time is then left on the tape. They can use the clock faces on PCM 17 if they find this difficult.

Average: Children may find it helpful to use the clock faces. They could set the clock at 12 o'clock, then move the hands for each programme that they choose, to help calculate the total time.

Less able: Children may find it helpful to use a clock face, moving just the minute hand to see how much time their chosen programmes last.

Optional adult input

Work with the Average group, helping them to calculate the total length of programmes, using a large teaching clock face.

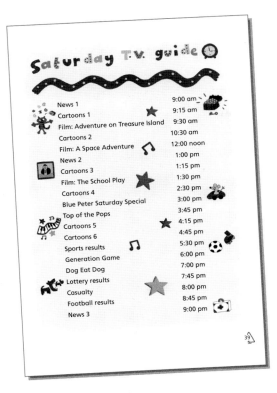

Saturday T.V. guide

News 1	9:00 am
Cartoons 1	9:15 am
Film: Adventure on Treasure Island	9:30 am
Cartoons 2	10:30 am
Film: A Space Adventure	12:00 noon
News 2	1:00 pm
Cartoons 3	1:15 pm
Film: The School Play	1:30 pm
Cartoons 4	2:30 pm
Blue Peter Saturday Special	3:00 pm
Top of the Pops	3:45 pm
Cartoons 5	4:15 pm
Cartoons 6	4:45 pm
Sports results	5:30 pm
Generation Game	6:00 pm
Dog Eat Dog	7:00 pm
Lottery results	7:45 pm
Casualty	8:00 pm
Football results	8:45 pm
News 3	9:00 pm

Plenary

1 Invite the Less able group to present their results. Use the teaching clock face to demonstrate the amount of time each programme lasts. Ask questions such as:

- *This programme starts at half past 5 and finishes at 6 o'clock. How long does the programme last?*

- *How much time is left on the video cassette? How did you work that out?*

- *Is there another way to fill an hour on the video cassette?*

Use the clock face to demonstrate the total amount of time taken, and encourage children to count in quarter hours and minutes. Ask children to offer different solutions, including, of course, a programme that lasts exactly an hour.

2 Repeat for children who had a 2-hour tape. Point out that, for this problem, the minute hand must pass around the clock twice in order to make 2 hours.

Ask children about the decisions they had to make. For example, if they had already used up 1 hour 15 minutes, then they could not record another 1-hour programme.

3 Repeat with the results from the 3-hour tape and ask:

- *How many times must the minute hand go around the clock to make 3 hours?*

Encourage children to explain how long 3 hours is, e.g. 180 minutes, 12 quarter hours . . .

Discuss how children recorded their results. Some may have drawn clock faces, others may have written lists or made a table to show how much time they have used. Encourage children to discuss the benefits of each method of recording and to suggest which they think would be best and why. All responses are acceptable, because the tabular recording, for example, would not be appropriate for all.

Some children may want to discuss 24-hour clock times. See **Useful mathematical information**, page 90, for a comparison chart.

Development

With parents' permission first, children could try this at home for real!

Solutions

A 15 mins	News 1 & 2, Cartoons 1 & 3, Lottery & Football results
B 30 mins	Cartoons 4 & 5, Top of the Pops, Sports results
C 45 mins	Blue Peter, Cartoons 6, Dog Eat Dog, Casualty
D 60 mins	All films, Generation Game
E 90 mins	Cartoons 2

One-hour tape possibilities
1 from **D**; 2 from **B**; 1 from **C** and 1 from **A**; 4 from **A**; 1 from **B** and 2 from **A**.

Two-hour tape possibilities
1 from **E** and 1 from **B**; 1 from **E** and 2 from **A**; 2 from **C** and 1 from **B**; any 2 one hour possibilities.

Three-hour tape possibilities
1 from **E**; 1 from **B** and any one hour possibility; 1 from **E**; 2 from **A** and any one hour possibility; 1 from **E** and 2 from **C**; any 3 one hour possibilities; 1 from **D** and any two hour possibility.

28 Ticker timer

Minimum prior experience

measuring the time taken using non-standard units;
More able: reading the time in seconds

Resources

coffee jar lids, card, scissors, glue, plasticine, paper for recording, stop clocks, different commercial sand timers, Textbook page 40

Key vocabulary

time, takes longer, takes less time, seconds

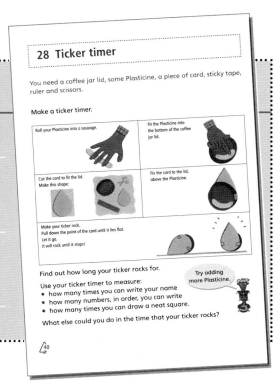

What's the problem?

Children make their own, non-standard timer, and they then try to work out for how long it will rock. They use it to measure everyday events in the classroom.

The tickers could be made as part of a design and technology project. The card pointer can be decorated, so that the ticker can be turned into, for example, a rocking Father Christmas, a Christmas tree, a clown . . . When the project has finished, children can take their tickers home.

Problem solving objectives

- Solve mathematical problems or puzzles, recognise simple patterns and relationships, generalise and predict. Suggest extensions by asking 'What if . . . ?' or 'What could I try next?'
- Explain how a problem was solved orally and, where appropriate, in writing.

Differentiation

The activity on Textbook page 40 is for the whole class, with differentiation by outcome.

Introducing the problem

Explain the problem to children: *Look in your books. Make a ticker timer like the one in the book. Then use your timer to find out how many things you can do while the ticker moves.*

Remind children that you would like them to record their results. Check that children understand how to make their timer and encourage them to begin this straight away.

Teacher focus for activity

All abilities: Ask children to use their timer to time events. Ask: *What else could you time? Why would that work?*

More able: Check that children understand how to measure the passing of time in seconds using a stop clock. They can then measure for how long their ticker rocks using a stop clock.

Average and Less able: Check that children understand that the sand timers measure time passing. They can compare how long their ticker rocks with a sand timer.

As children work, ask questions, such as:

- *Which lasts longer, the sand running through the sand timer or your ticker?*
- *Which measures a longer length of time? How did you work that out?*
- *What else could you time with your ticker?*

Work with the More able group. Check that they understand how to read seconds on a stop clock.

Plenary

1 Invite various children to explain how they worked out how long their timer rocked. Methods could include:

- comparing their ticker with different sand timers to find the nearest;

- measuring as accurately as they can with a stop clock;

- counting seconds, perhaps by saying 'One one thousand, two one thousand . . . ' (see also **Useful mathematical information**, page 90).

2 Discuss the different methods used. Invite the More able group to demonstrate how to use the stop clock to measure time. Ask children to evaluate these methods. Encourage them to consider how accurate each method was. Note that home-made tickers like these rarely rock for much more than about 10 seconds. Discuss whether children were able to make the tickers rock for a longer time.

3 Ask pairs to give their results for how many times they could write their name before the ticker stopped. Ask:

- *Why are the results not all the same?*

Responses could include:

- different numbers of letters in a name;

- speed of writing;

- how many seconds the ticker rocked for.

Ask 'ticker time' questions, such as:

- *If you wrote your name 8 times in 1 'ticker time', how many times could you write it in 5 'ticker times'?*

Repeat this for the other measures that children made.

4 Ask children to show how they recorded their results. They may have:

- drawn pictures to show what they could do in the given time;

- written a list;

- made a simple table.

Discuss the benefits of each method of recording.

5 Ask children to estimate how many ticks it would take to draw a circle, then check by trying. Ask:

- *What was your estimate? And your check?*

- *Did everyone have the same result? Why not?*

Discuss the importance of using standard units of time for measuring time passing.

6 Finally, ask children to suggest some other ideas for what they could use their ticker to measure. Where practicable, children could try these out.

29 Sand weight challenge

Minimum prior experience

weighing in grams; balancing using a 2-pan balance; understanding of multiples of 10

Resources

small sandwich bags and ties, dry sand, 20g weights, 50g weights, 2-pan balances, gummed labels, paper for recording, a fairly accurate dial or digital balance, Textbook page 41

Key vocabulary

weigh, weighs, balances, heavy/light, heavier/lighter, gram, balance, scales, weight, method

29 Sand weight challenge

This is a special weighing and balancing challenge.

You need some sand, small bags, bag ties, labels, several 20g and 50g weights and a 2-pan balance.

Try to make bags of sand that weigh:

❶ 20g
❷ 40g
❸ 50g
❹ 100g
❺ 10g
❻ 30g
❼ 60g
❽ 70g
❾ 80g
❿ 90g

What weights can you make with 50g and 20g? Try making a list.

Remember, you can only use your 20g and 50g weights to help you each time.

Hmm... How can you make 10g using 20g weights?

41

What's the problem?

This investigation involves combining weights, halving quantities to make new amounts and an understanding of multiples of 20 and 50.

Problem solving objectives

- Choose and use appropriate operations and efficient calculation strategies to solve problems.
- Solve mathematical problems or puzzles, recognise simple patterns and relationships, generalise and predict. Suggest extensions by asking 'What if . . . ?' or 'What could I try next?'
- Explain how a problem was solved orally and, where appropriate, in writing.
- Solve word problems involving measures.

Differentiation

More able: Textbook page 41, problems 5–10.

Average: Textbook page 41, problems 2–6.

Less able: Textbook page 41, problems 1–4.

Introducing the problem

Explain the problem to children: *Your task is to find a way of filling these bags to the weights shown in the Textbook. However, you can only use 50 gram and 20 gram weights, and 2-pan balances to do this.*

Check that children understand what to do. Remind them to close their finished sand-bag weights with a bag tie and to label them with their weight. Suggest that they discuss the problem with their partner and decide how they will work.

Teacher focus for activity

All abilities: Ask questions such as:

- *How will you do this?*
- *What do you think you need to do first?*

More able: Encourage children to work out some addition and subtraction sentences to show possible solutions. Suggest to children that they search for more than one way of making the sand weights. Ask children to think about how they will record their work. They may decide to use the calculations that they have devised.

Average: Discuss with children how they can make the sand weights, and encourage them to write some simple addition and subtraction sentences to show this. Ask children to think about how they will record what they have done. They may write number sentences or decide to draw pictures to show what they did.

Less able: Children can pour out sand to balance the 20g and 50g weights. For 40g and 100g, they will find it helpful to think about doubles. Ask: *How will you record what you have done?* Children may decide to draw some pictures or to write number sentences.

As children work, ask questions, such as:

- *How did you work that out?*
- *Is there another way of making that weight?*

Optional adult input

Work with the More able group. Encourage them to find different ways to make each weight.

Plenary

1 On the board, write the weights to be made, in order, from 10g to 100g, in a column (see **Useful mathematical information**, page 90, for a discussion about the difference between mass and weight).

10g	
20g	One 20g weight
30g	
40g	2 × 20g weights 20g + 20g = 40g
50g	One 50g weight

2 Invite some of the Less able group to explain how they made their weights of 20g, 40g, 50g and 100g. On the chart, write in their solutions and, where an addition or subtraction has been used, show this too.

Ask the other children:

- *Can you think of another way of working these out?*

- *Which way is the simpler to do? Why is that?*

3 Invite children to weigh some of their bags of sand and to check how accurate they were. Where there are discrepancies in the weights, invite children to suggest reasons for this. These could include:

- the 2-pan balance was out of balance;

- the sand was not weighed or balanced carefully enough;

- the bag, tie and label add to the weight.

4 Take the solutions from the other 2 groups in the same way, continuing to complete the chart on the board and allowing children to check the weights of their bags. Discuss the calculations and recording methods used. Say:

- *Did you write number sentences? How did this help you?*

- *How did you record your work? Which way is easier to read?*

Congratulate children on their work, as they will have had to use many different skills in order to solve their problems.

Solutions

Combinations to make 10g, 20g, 30g, 40g, 50g, 60g, 70g, 80g, 90g and 100g.

The following table shows a possible way of making each weight. Children may well have alternative methods that also are valid.

Weight	Method 1
10g	Weigh out 20g, using a 20g weight, then share this evenly between 2 pans so that they balance. $20g \div 2 = 10g$
20g	Weigh out 20g, using a 20g weight.
30g	Weigh out 50g. Pour out 20g. What is left is 30g of sand. $50g - 20g = 30g$
40g	Weigh 20g twice, to make 40g. $20g + 20g = 40g$
50g	Weigh out 50g, using a 50g weight.
60g	Weigh out $3 \times 20g$ to make 60g. $20g + 20g + 20g = 60g$
70g	Weigh out 20g plus 50g. $20g + 50g = 70g$
80g	Weigh out $4 \times 20g$. $20g + 20g + 20g + 20g = 80g$
90g	Weigh out 50g plus 20g plus 20g. $50g + 20g + 20g = 90g$
100g	Weigh out 50g plus 50g. $50g + 50g = 100g$ Or combine $5 \times 20g$. $20g + 20g + 20g + 20g + 20g = 100g$

30 Hoop roll

Minimum prior experience

estimating and measuring in metres and centimetres

Resources

small, medium and large PE hoops, quoits, measuring tapes, metre sticks, chalk, felt pens, large sheets of paper, paper for recording, Textbook page 42

Key vocabulary

length, long, far, further, furthest, distance apart . . . between . . . to . . . from, ruler, metre stick, tape measure, string, method

What's the problem?

Children estimate and measure the circumferences of circular objects.

Problem solving objectives

- Solve mathematical problems or puzzles, recognise simple patterns and relationships, generalise and predict. Suggest extensions by asking 'What if . . . ?' or 'What could I try next?'
- Explain how a problem was solved orally and, where appropriate, in writing.
- Solve word problems involving measures.

Differentiation

The activity on Textbook page 42 is for the whole class, with differentiation by outcome. As the Textbook contains a hint, you may wish to give this only to the Less able group.

Introducing the problem

Explain the problem: *Sam and Shefali were rolling hoops on the playground. They wondered how far a hoop would roll in one turn.* Suggest to children that they devise their method, using quoits, in the classroom, and then, when everyone is ready, you will all go out into the playground to use hoops, so that there is plenty of room to carry out the investigation. Children should try this experiment for different-sized hoops, as well as for the quoits.

Establish that you are particularly interested in how they tackle this problem. Point out to children the resources that you have made available so that they can begin by thinking about how to carry out the investigation. Check that children are clear about how they might record their results. Some may suggest marking the start and finish of the hoop roll on large sheets of paper, and measuring that; others that they will mark this on the playground. Ask them to write some sentences explaining what they did and their results.

Teacher focus for activity

All abilities: Establish that children have devised a method. Encourage children to estimate first how far the hoop will roll. Ask questions such as: *What do you need to solve this problem? What have you done so far? What will you do next?*

More able: Check that children have considered how to tell where the start of a roll is; children may suggest chalking a point on the hoop to do this. Discuss their estimate, and how they thought this through. Encourage children to use a tabular form of recording, which includes both their estimate and measure.

Object	Estimate	Measure
Large hoop	2 metres 50 centimetres	3 metres 15 centimetres

Average: Ask: *Which units do you think you will use for measuring?* Check that their answer is sensible. Ask: *How far do you think the hoop will roll?* Discuss their thinking about this.

Less able: Establish that children have a working method that they can explain and demonstrate using a quoit. Children may find it easier to cut a length of string to the length of the hoop roll, then measure the length of the string.

Ask questions as children work, such as:

- *What units are you using? Why did you choose those?*
- *What is your estimate?*

Optional adult input

Work with the Less able group and encourage children to use the language of measures to explain what they plan to do.

Plenary

1 Begin with the quoit and invite children from different groups to explain what they decided to do. Methods could include:

- making a mark with chalk on the quoit, then rolling the quoit on paper, from a starting line, beginning and ending with the mark on the quoit touching the paper;

- outside in the playground, either marking start and finish lines on large sheets of paper or directly onto the playground with chalk;
- using a tape measure to measure the distance of the roll directly;
- cutting a length of string to find the distance between the 2 marks, then measuring the string directly along a metre stick.

A further method that children may have considered is to measure the distance around the hoop directly by:

- placing a length of string around the hoop, and measuring the string;
- using a measuring tape around the circumference.

Measuring the circumference of the hoop would demonstrate that children understood that one turn of the hoop was the same measurement as the circumference of the hoop. This is not always obvious to children. (Decide whether to use the word **circumference**.) However, other children may also have realised this, but decided to use the rolling method. (It is easier to do!) See also **Useful mathematical information**, page 90, for further information on finding circumferences.

2 Discuss with children how well their methods worked, and encourage them to evaluate the effectiveness of what they did. Ask questions, such as:

- *Which method do you think is easier to do? Why do you think that?*
- *Which units did you choose for your estimate and measure? Why did you make this choice?*

3 Where children have not made the connection between the circumference and roll lengths, ask:

- *What do you think the hoop measures all the way around?*

Then check this by asking 2 children to measure the hoop and then to measure one roll.

4 Invite various children to show how they recorded their results. Discuss their estimates and measures and how close these were. Invite children to discuss which method of recording they preferred and why.

Development

Children could repeat this investigation using cylinders that they find at home, such as baked bean tins, plastic bottles . . .

Useful mathematical information

These pages provide further explanation of the mathematics used in each lesson. Each section is referenced to the relevant activity so that it is easy to find what is needed starting from the lesson plan for the problem.

Some sections cover the mathematics that underpins the problem. Other sections cover specific mathematical concepts that children will need to understand. Both are intended to be information for the non-specialist mathematics teacher.

1 Frame it!

Perimeters

Where the frame of a square is considered, the number patterns do not produce square numbers because the square is not completely filled in. It is the sides of the square that are considered, or its perimeter. In order to consider the total number of cubes used, counting how many in each side would mean that some cubes are counted twice.

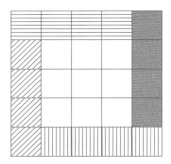

In order to make a square, the total number of cubes used for the perimeter must be divisible exactly by 4.

2 Number line

To make each numeral in the numbers 1 to 100, the same amount of each digit is required, apart from zero and one.

Look at the following 100 square. Each digit, except '0' and '1', is needed 10 times for when it is used as the units digit, and 10 times for when it is used as the tens digit. This can be seen clearly if highlighted on a 100 square, remembering to count the crossover

point twice. Ask children to predict what the crossover point for each digit will be. (11, 22, 33, 44 . . .)

1	2	3	4	5	6	7	8	9	10
11	12	13	14	15	16	17	18	19	20
21	22	23	24	25	26	27	28	29	30
31	32	33	34	35	36	37	38	39	40
41	42	43	44	45	46	47	48	49	50
51	53	53	54	55	56	57	58	59	60
61	63	63	64	65	66	67	68	69	70
71	72	73	74	75	76	77	78	79	80
81	82	83	84	85	86	87	88	89	90
91	92	93	94	95	96	97	98	99	100

If the unit numbers 1 to 9 were written with zero in front of the unit (01, 02, 03 . . .) then 20 of each digit would be required, except for '1', which also needs an extra digit for '100'.

3 How old is Granny?

Totalling odd and even numbers

When totalling 2 odd numbers the result is always even:

$3 + 5 = 8$

The number sentence could be rewritten as:

$(2 + 1) + (4 + 1)$ or $2 + 4 + 1 + 1 = 2 + 4 + 2$

From this, it can be seen that each odd number is 1 more than an even number, so that the total will always be even.

However, if totalling 3 odd numbers, the total will always be odd:

$3 + 5 + 7 = 15$ or $(2 + 1) + (4 + 1) + (6 + 1)$

Here there is an odd 1, so that the result will be odd.

When totalling 2 even numbers, the result will always be even because there is no 'odd' unpaired 1.

When totalling an odd and an even number, the result will always be odd, because the odd number is 1 more than an even number:

$3 + 4$
$(2 + 1) + 4 = 2 + 4 + 1 = 6 + 1$

4 Number generator

Place value

Where there are 2 different digits, it is possible to make two 2-digit numbers,

e.g. 1 and 2 make 12 and 21.

Where there are 3 different digits, it is possible to make six 3-digit numbers,

e.g. 2, 4 and 6 make 246, 264, 426, 462, 624 and 642.

Where there are 4 different digits, it is possible to make twenty-four 4-digit numbers, e.g. 3, 5, 7, 9: 3579, 3597, 3759, 3795, 3957, 3975, 5379, 5397, 5739, 5793, 5937, 5973, 7359, 7395, 7539, 7593, 7935, 7953, 9357, 9375, 9537, 9573, 9735 and 9753.

The amount of possible numbers increases dramatically, the more digits that there are.

However, if zero is one of the given digits, this will in each case alter the amount of numbers that can be made, because we do not use the zero to show an empty tens position in single-digit numbers such as 1, 2, 3 . . . or to show an empty hundreds place in 2-digit numbers such as 45, 64, 31 . . .

5 Next-door numbers

Consecutive numbers

It is always possible to write an odd number as the sum of two consecutive numbers. For example:
$15 = 7 + 8$, $151 = 75 + 76$, $369 = 184 + 185$ . . .

Consecutive numbers can be found by dividing any odd number by 2:

$151 \div 2 = 75$ remainder 1
So $151 = 75 + 75 + 1$ or $75 + 76$

Powers of 2 cannot be written as consecutive numbers. These can all be made by even doubles:

$4 = 2 + 2$
$8 = 4 + 4$
$16 = 8 + 8$
$64 = 32 + 32$ . . .

Sums of 3 consecutive numbers are all multiples of 3:

$15 = 4 + 5 + 6$
$21 = 6 + 7 + 8$ . . .

Sums of 5 consecutive numbers are all multiples of 5:

$15 = 1 + 2 + 3 + 4 + 5$
$25 = 3 + 4 + 5 + 6 + 7$ . . .

Numbers that are the sum of 2 or more consecutive whole numbers are called 'Polite numbers'.

6 What's the rule?

There are many different number sets to be found in mathematics. Some of these can be expressed using signs.

For example, for 'is greater than', the statement *10 is greater than 1, 2, 3, 4, 5* . . . can be written:

$10 > (1, 2, 3, 4, 5, 6, 7, 8$ or $9)$

and for 'is less than', the statement *10 is less than 11, 12, 13* . . . can be written:

$10 < (11, 12, 13, 14, 15 \ldots)$

Practice in recognising the properties of different numbers and the relationships between them will be valuable to children as they start to carry out more complex calculations and use larger and larger numbers.

7 Fraction flags

There are many different ways of showing fractions on a grid. For example, if the grid had four squares, and a $\frac{1}{4}$ has to be shown by shading squares, there would be four different ways of showing that. If $\frac{1}{2}$ had to be shown on a 2×2 grid, then again there would be a number of solutions:

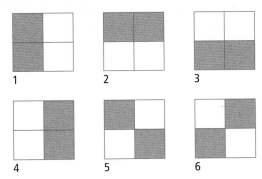

1   2   3

4   5   6

Some of these solutions could be regarded as 'the same': grids 1 to 4 are reflections or rotations of each other, and grid 6 is a rotation or reflection of grid 5.

Children do need to understand that a fraction of a shape or a set is an equal part. For example, $\frac{1}{5}$ of 35 is 7, where the number 35 is divided into 5 equal parts.

For fractions of shapes, a common misconception is that the shape can be divided into unequal parts. For example, a child might show $\frac{1}{3}$ of a circle

like this: instead of this:

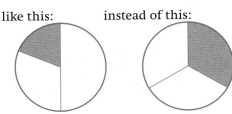

8 Dart totals

Associative law

The associative law for addition states that it does not matter which pair of numbers are added first. For example:

$$20 + 19 + 18 = 20 + (19 + 18) = (20 + 19) + 18$$

So, in activity 8, where the numbers to be totalled are in a different order, it is, in fact, the same sum.

Multiplication is associative: that is, it does not matter in which order the numbers are multiplied.

Subtraction and division are not associative, and the order of the operation does matter. For example, for $10 - 5 - 2$:

$$(10 - 5) - 2 = 5 - 2 = 3$$
$$10 - (5 - 2) = 10 - 3 = 7$$

Commutative law

Children also need to understand commutativity. That is, for any two numbers being added, it does not matter in which order they are added. So, $3 + 5 = 5 + 3$

Multiplication is commutative, e.g. $5 \times 3 = 3 \times 5$

Subtraction and division are not commutative: $5 - 3$ does not give the same answer as $3 - 5$

9 Arithmagons

Arithmagons are useful devices for exploring addition problems. They can be as simple as:

> The arithmagon uses all of the numbers 1, 2, 3, 4, 5 and 6.
> Each side has the same total.
> Write in the missing numbers.

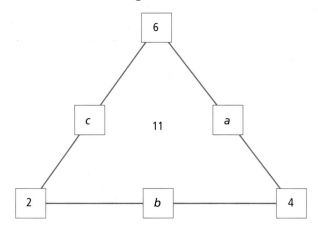

Arithmagons can show algebraic relationships. If the total of each side is given, then in the example where the total is 11:

$$11 - (6 + 4) = a \qquad 11 - (4 + 2) = b \qquad 11 - (2 + 6) = c$$
$$a = 1 \qquad\qquad b = 5 \qquad\qquad c = 3$$

10 Four in a row

Empty number line

The empty number line is a useful device for calculating addition and subtraction. Children can use this as a way of visualising the operation that they are performing.

For example:

$$34 + 58$$

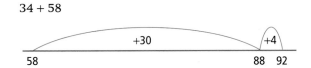

In the above example, the child begins with the larger number, 58, then adds 30 and then 4. This could be broken down even further into add 30, add 2 (to make 90) and then add 2.

Similarly, this method can be used for subtraction.

For $96 - 37$:

This could be broken down further into $96 - 30$, then $66 - 6$ and then $60 - 1$.

11 Square numbers

Addition of diagonal numbers in a hundred square

Addition of diagonal numbers in any different diagonals in any square within a 100 square always gives the same answer.

Look at the squares on the next page. Each of the pairs of numbers contains the same units and tens but in different numbers, for example $1 + 12$ and $2 + 11$ both contain 1 and 2 and 10, and $15 + 37$ and $17 + 35$ both contain 10, 5, 7 and 30. The additions therefore give the same totals.

1 + 12 = 13
11 + 2 = 13

15 + 37 = 52
17 + 35 = 52

In the 3 × 3 square, the central column and row also give the same answer: 16 + 36 = 52 and 25 + 27 = 52. This is because all four lines intersect in '26'. The total is always double the middle number, e.g. double 26 = 52. However, in the 4 × 4 square, the vertical and horizontal lines do not give the same total, because there is no common intersection for the lines and so no symmetry of the digits in the numbers.

56	57	58	59
66	67	68	69
76	77	78	79
86	87	88	89

56 + 89 = 145
86 + 59 = 145

The same is true of rectangles within a 100 square.

| 15 | 16 | 17 | 18 |
| 25 | 26 | 27 | 28 |

15 + 28 = 43
18 + 25 = 43

12 Solve it!

Differences

When considering whole positive numbers, the following rules always apply:

- The difference between two odd numbers is always even.

  Think of **any** 2 odd numbers that are reasonably close together, such as 9 and 15. The difference is 6, which is an even number.

- The difference between 2 even numbers is always even.

  Think of **any** 2 even numbers, such as 8 and 16. The difference is 8, which is an even number.

- The difference between any odd number and any even number is always odd.

  Think of **any** odd and **any** even numbers, such as 8 and 11. The difference is 3, which is an odd number.

13 Equal totals

In order to solve this problem, and to use one each of 3, 4, 5 and 6 in each row, column and diagonal, children need to understand the associative law (see activity 8 in this section, page 84). The law states that for addition, it does not matter in which order the numbers are totalled.

Consider this solution to the puzzle:

4	6	3	5
3	5	4	6
5	3	6	4
6	4	5	3

Here, each row, column and diagonal has one each of 3, 4, 5 and 6; however, the order in which they are written differs in each one.

14 Make fifteen

Making totals of 10, using the digits 1 to 9

There are more ways of making 10 using 2 digits each time than of making other 2-digit totals.

1 + 9 = 10
2 + 8 = 10
3 + 7 = 10
4 + 6 = 10
(5 + 5 = 10; not possible in the game, as there is only one 5 card)
6 + 4 = 10
7 + 3 = 10
8 + 2 = 10
9 + 1 = 10

In this game, if the first player takes the '5' card, then a pair of cards that totals 10, then they will win. Children who know their number bonds to 10 can use this fact to develop a winning strategy. Similarly, they can use the strategy to stop their partner from winning, by taking for themselves whichever complement to make 10 their partner needs to win.

15 Counter shapes

Number rectangles

Prime numbers will only make a single-row rectangle – that is, 1 multiplied by itself; for example, 5 gives 1 × 5 and 13 gives 1 × 13.

Rectangular numbers are numbers that can be represented by dots arranged to form an array; for example, 12, which is 6×2 and 4×3.

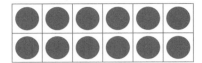

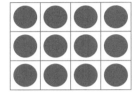

Square numbers are special rectangular numbers that make arrays in which both numbers are the same; for example, 25, which is 5×5.

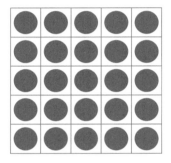

16 Two-dice totals

Probability

When tossing two 1 to 6 dice and adding the scores, the possibilities of making the different totals are not the same. The most likely total is 7.

Total	Scores						Number of possible ways
1	No solution possible						0
2	1 + 1						1
3	1 + 2	2 + 1					2
4	1 + 3	2 + 2	3 + 1				3
5	1 + 4	2 + 3	3 + 2	4 + 1			4
6	1 + 5	2 + 4	3 + 3	4 + 2	5 + 1		5
7	1 + 6	2 + 5	3 + 4	4 + 3	5 + 2	6 + 1	6
8	2 + 6	3 + 5	4 + 4	5 + 3	6 + 2		5
9	3 + 6	4 + 5	5 + 4	6 + 3			4
10	4 + 6	5 + 5	6 + 4				3
11	5 + 6	6 + 5					2
12	6 + 6						1
13	No solution possible						0

It is possible to make the total 7 in six different ways. Think about any 1 to 6 dice. The opposite sides always total 7, so:

$$1 + 6 = 7$$
$$2 + 5 = 7$$
$$3 + 4 = 7$$
$$4 + 3 = 7$$
$$5 + 2 = 7$$
$$6 + 1 = 7$$

The table of probabilities is symmetrical, so that there is only one way of making 2 and 12, two ways of making 3 and 11, and so on.

17 Animal quackers

Combinations of multiples of 2 and 4

Multiples of 2 and multiples of 4 are always even, and all multiples of 4 are also multiples of 2, but not, of course, the other way around. In this problem, this gives rise to some interesting number patterns.

Look at the following table, which shows ways of totalling 32 using combinations of multiples of 2 and multiples of 4.

Multiples of 4	Multiples of 2	Number sentence
0	16	$(0 \times 4) + (16 \times 2) = 32$
1	14	$(1 \times 4) + (14 \times 2) = 32$
2	12	$(2 \times 4) + (12 \times 2) = 32$
3	10	$(3 \times 4) + (10 \times 2) = 32$
4	8	$(4 \times 4) + (8 \times 2) = 32$
5	6	$(5 \times 4) + (6 \times 2) = 32$
6	4	$(6 \times 4) + (4 \times 2) = 32$
7	2	$(7 \times 4) + (2 \times 2) = 32$
8	0	$(8 \times 4) + (0 \times 2) = 32$

Note that it is not possible to have a combination with an odd number of 2s. This is because it would always leave a difference of 2 from the total 32.

On the other hand, it is possible to have an odd number of 4s, because an even number of 2s would provide another number in the 4 times table. For example,

3×4 and 10×2 give
12 and 20,
making a total of 32

Note that 20, which is a multiple of 2, is also a multiple of 4.

18 Digits

Multiplying by 5, 10 and 20

There are close links between the 5, 10 and 20 times tables because 10 is 5×2 and 20 is 5×4 and 10×2.

Multiples of 5	Multiples of 10	Multiples of 20
$1 \times 5 = 5$		
$2 \times 5 = 10$	$1 \times 10 = 10$	
$3 \times 5 = 15$		
$4 \times 5 = 20$	$2 \times 10 = 20$	$1 \times 20 = 20$
$5 \times 5 = 25$		
$6 \times 5 = 30$	$3 \times 10 = 30$	
$7 \times 5 = 35$		
$8 \times 5 = 40$	$4 \times 10 = 40$	$2 \times 20 = 40$
$9 \times 5 = 45$		
$10 \times 5 = 50$	$5 \times 10 = 50$	
$11 \times 5 = 55$		
$12 \times 5 = 60$	$6 \times 10 = 60$	$3 \times 20 = 60$

19 Pocket money

Combinations

Imagine that you have some counters, which are labelled A, B, C, . . .

First take 3 counters: A, B, C. You can choose 2 each time. So you can choose:

A and B
A and C
B and C

There are 3 possible ways of choosing.

This time take 6 counters. You can choose 5 each time.

A B C D E
A B C D F
A B C E F
A B D E F
A C D E F
B C D E F

There are 5 possible ways of choosing.

20 Leapfrog

Multiples of 2 and 3

Where a multiple of 2 and a multiple of 3 coincide, they produce a multiple of 6.

Where a multiple of 3 and a multiple of 4 coincide, they produce a multiple of 12.

For example:

	Multiple of 2	Multiple of 3	Multiple of 4	Multiple of 6	Multiple of 12
1					
2	✓				
3		✓			
4	✓		✓		
5					
6	✓	✓		✓	
7					
8	✓		✓		
9		✓			
10	✓				
11					
12	✓	✓	✓	✓	✓
13					
14	✓				
15		✓			
16	✓		✓		
17					
18	✓	✓		✓	
19					
20	✓		✓		

This can also be shown by plotting multiples on a number line or 100 square.

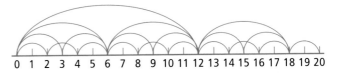

21 Make a shape

Where 2 shape tiles have at least one side that has the same length, the following matching of sides are possible.

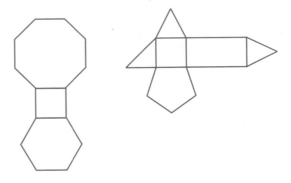

In order to place 2 shapes together in the correct orientation, children will need to have a good command of shape, position and direction language.

Try describing one of the composite shapes above to another adult. Ask them to draw what you say. Then swap over, so that you now draw from their verbal instructions. What is important in activities like this is the accuracy of the verbal instructions – how carefully and accurately each shape and its position are described.

22 Shape pairs

Symmetry

This can be imagined as a reflection of half of the shape in a mirror, with the mirror line passing directly through the shape.

For example:

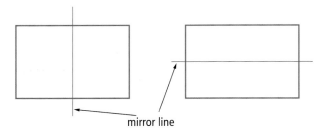

mirror line

The mirror line can be imagined in the horizontal or vertical position.

Patterns on peg boards, or with coloured interlocking cubes, that are symmetrical can also be made. Some patterns, or shapes, will have 2 or more lines of symmetry, for example:

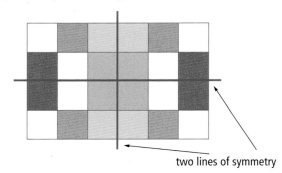

two lines of symmetry

23 Cube shapes

Traditionally, activities that involve making shapes use square tiles. That is, the results have a '2-D' effect. One side of a square must completely touch another side of another square, so that, for example, a result such as the following would not count:

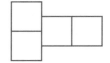

With 4 squares, it is possible to make 5 shapes.

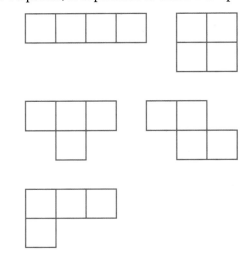

With 3 squares, it is possible to make the following 2 shapes:

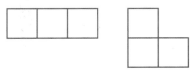

Using interlocking cubes and a third dimension introduces further possibilities if more than 3 cubes are used. For example, 8 shapes can be made using 4 cubes.

24 Four-sided shapes

4-sided flat, or plane, shapes are called quadrilaterals, or 4-sided polygons. These include:

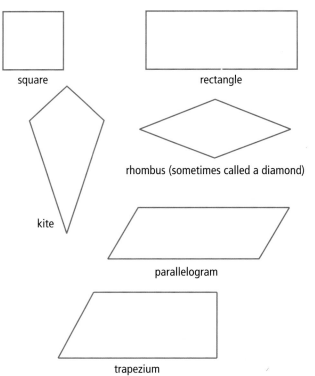

square

rectangle

kite

rhombus (sometimes called a diamond)

parallelogram

trapezium

25 Four the same

This problem considers trying to fill a 4 × 4 grid with each of these shapes:

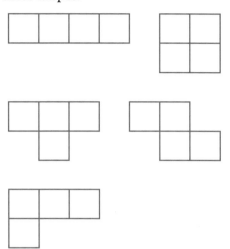

The problem can be extended by filling an enlarged 16-square version of each of the shapes below with the 4-cube shapes.

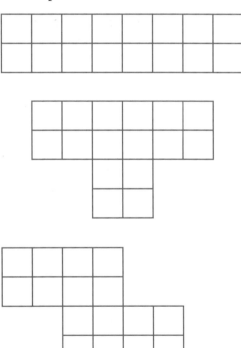

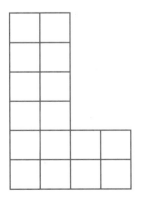

26 Triangle trap

Triangles

There are various forms of triangle.

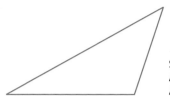

Scalene
All 3 sides are different lengths.
All 3 angles are different sizes.

Isosceles
Two sides are the same length, and different from the third.
The 2 angles formed by the equal sides and the base are equal.

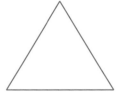

Equilateral
All 3 sides are equal in length.
All 3 angles measure 60°.

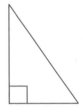

Right-angled triangle
Contains 1 angle that measures 90°.

Isosceles and scalene triangles can have 1 obtuse angle – that is, 1 angle that is greater than 90° and less than 180°. Right-angled and equilateral triangles cannot have an obtuse angle.

27 Favourite TV programmes

Children may raise the issue of 24-hour clocks, as most will have seen these – perhaps on their video recorder, or cooker clock, at home.

The following table gives the relationship between time recorded in 12-hour time and in 24-hour time.

12-hour clock	24-hour clock	12-hour clock	24-hour clock
12 am or midnight	00:00	12 pm or noon	12:00
1 am	01:00	1 pm	13:00
2 am	02:00	2 pm	14:00
3 am	03:00	3 pm	15:00
4 am	04:00	4 pm	16:00
5 am	05:00	5 pm	17:00
6 am	06:00	6 pm	18:00
7 am	07:00	7 pm	19:00
8 am	08:00	8 pm	20:00
9 am	09:00	9 pm	21:00
10 am	10:00	10 pm	22:00
11 am	11:00	11 pm	23:00

28 Ticker timer

Counting in seconds

People have tried many ways to estimate time in seconds. Here are two of them:

- One elephant, two elephants, three elephants . . .
- One one thousand, two one thousand, three one thousand . . .

These ways are often used during a thunderstorm to calculate roughly how far away the centre of the storm is. As soon as the lightening is seen, begin to count the seconds. As soon as the thunder is heard, stop counting. The last number in the count gives a rough idea of how many miles away the storm centre is.

29 Sand weight challenge

There is much discussion about the difference between mass and weight. Here are some definitions:

- Mass is the amount of matter in something and is always the same, whether the object is on Earth or out in space.
- Weight is the force with which the object is attracted to Earth. In space, an object would have no weight because the forces exerted on it by other stars and planets balance out the force of gravity from Earth.

The problem can be adapted for other measures, for example:

- Use 20 cm and 50 cm of string to measure lengths between 10 cm and 100 cm, in 10 cm increments.
- Use 20 cl and 50 cl containers to fill a container with between 10 cl and 100 cl of water, in 10 cl increments.

30 Hoop roll

Circumferences

One turn of a car wheel is the same distance as the circumference of the wheel.

To find the circumference of a circle, you will need to know its radius or diameter. (The diameter is twice the radius.)

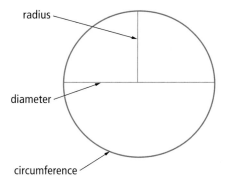

The formula for finding the circumference of a circle is:

- $2\pi r$ or πd

where r is the radius, d is the diameter and π is $\frac{22}{7}$ or approximately 3.142.

It is interesting to note that there seems to be some confusion in the general population about the circumference of wheels. The wheel of a car is the metal hub. Wheels are measured not by their circumference, but by the diameter of the hub. If you are trying to calculate the rolling circumference of the wheel and the tyre, you need to include the width of the tyre as well as the diameter of the hub.

During a foot and mouth epidemic, some farmers put down a very narrow strip of disinfected straw for their vehicles to cross. The width of the straw may have represented the diameter of the hub, but the total rolling circumference is more than three times the size of the diameter of the wheel plus the tyre, so the strip of straw was not wide enough to disinfect the entire circumference of the tyre.

0	1	2	3	4	5	6	7	8
9	10	11	12	13	14	15	16	17
18	19	20	21	22	23	24	25	26
27	28	29	30	31	32	33	34	35
36	37	38	39	40	41	42	43	44
45	46	47	48	49	50	51	52	53

0–53 Number line

1

47	48	49	50	51	52	53	54	55
56	57	58	59	60	61	62	63	64
65	66	67	68	69	70	71	72	73
74	75	76	77	78	79	80	81	82
83	84	85	86	87	88	89	90	91
92	93	94	95	96	97	98	99	100

47–100 Number line

2

Hundred square

1	2	3	4	5	6	7	8	9	10
11	12	13	14	15	16	17	18	19	20
21	22	23	24	25	26	27	28	29	30
31	32	33	34	35	36	37	38	39	40
41	42	43	44	45	46	47	48	49	50
51	52	53	54	55	56	56	58	59	60
61	62	63	64	65	66	67	68	69	70
71	72	73	74	75	76	77	78	79	80
81	82	83	84	85	86	87	88	89	90
91	92	93	94	95	96	97	98	99	100

Digit cards

(4)

4

9

3

8

2

7

1

6

0

5

Three-spike abacus

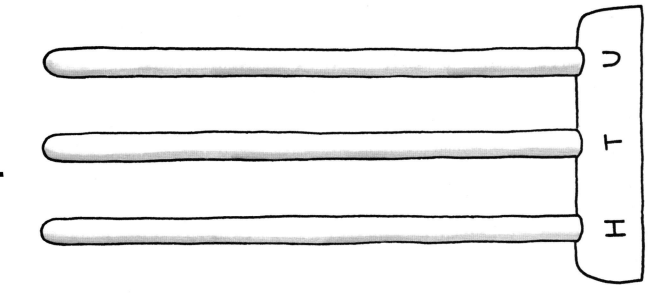

Two-spike abacus

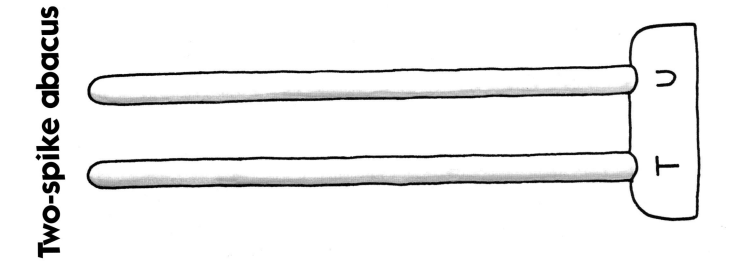

Fraction flags 1

Shade in squares to record your flags.

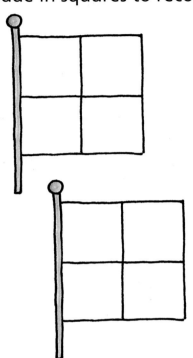
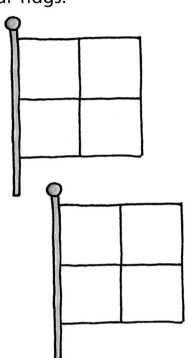
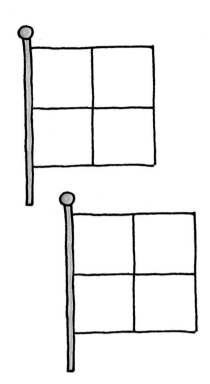

Fraction flags 2

Shade in squares to record your flags.

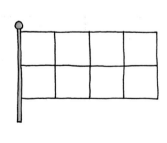
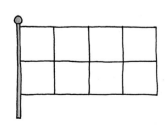
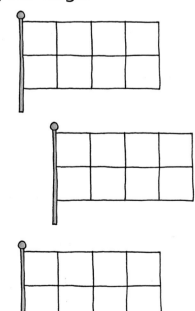
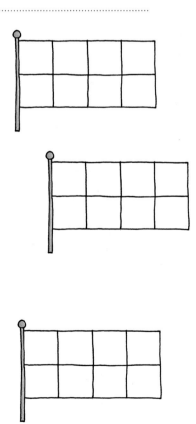

Fraction flags 3

Shade in squares to record your flags.

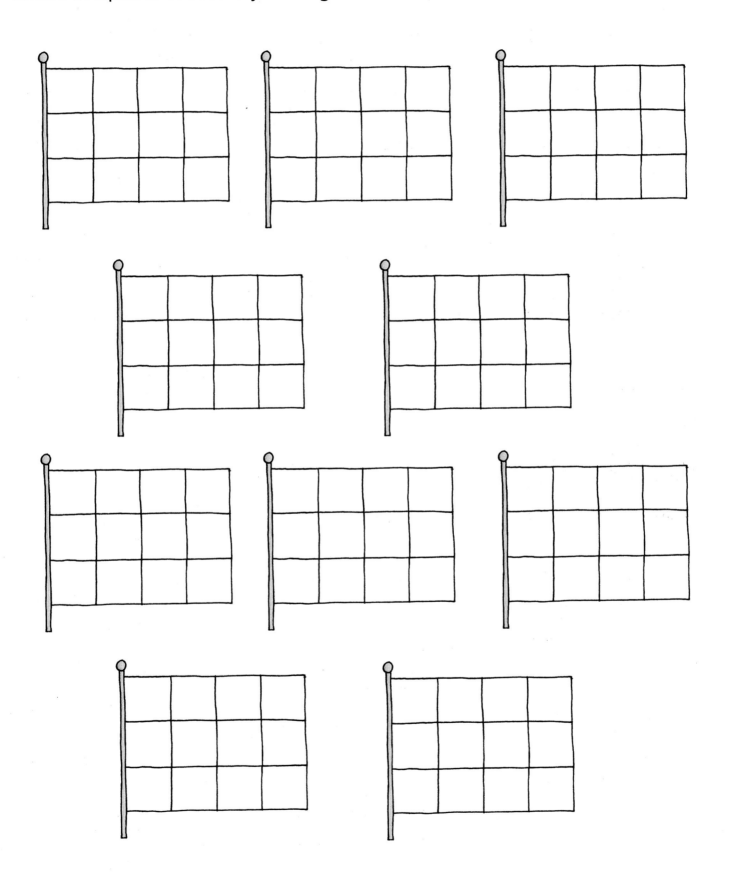

Dart totals

Record your darts. Write the total.

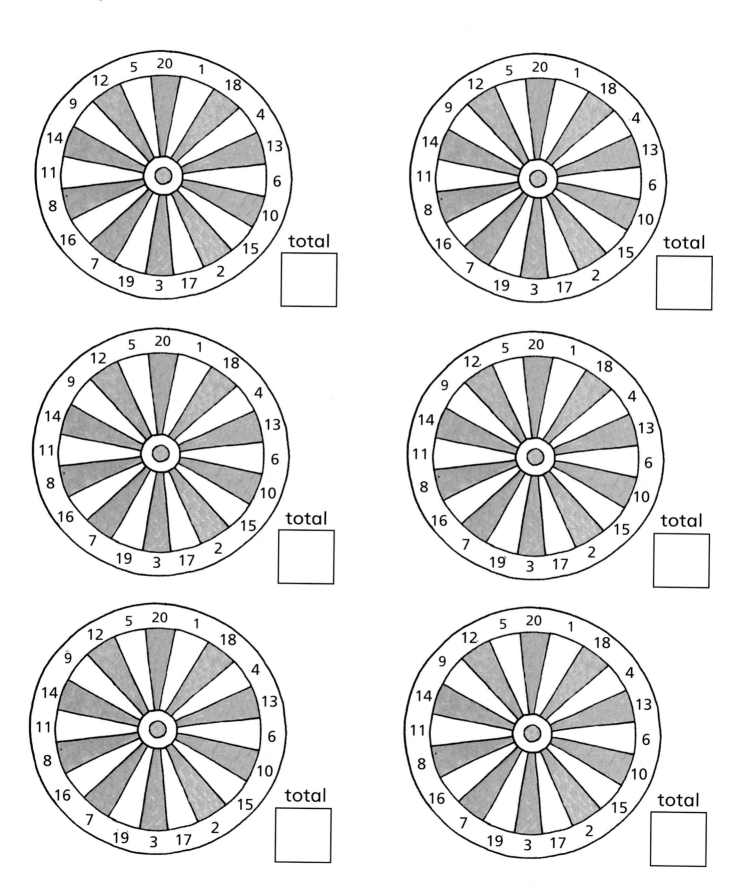

Arithmagons

Record your arithmagon solutions here

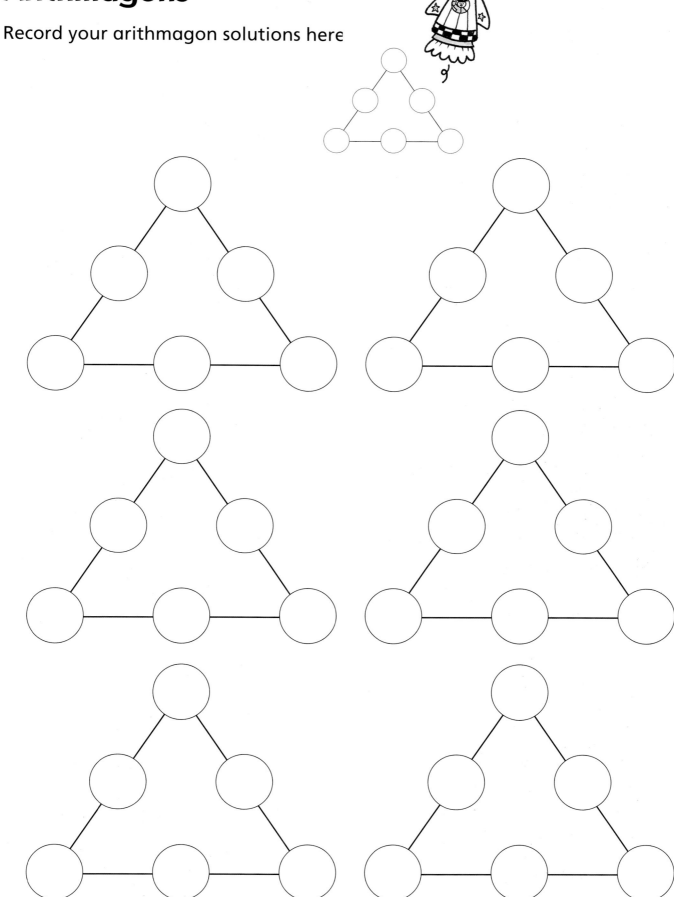

Four in a row

Make up your own 'Four in a row' game.

Play your game with a friend.

Numbers

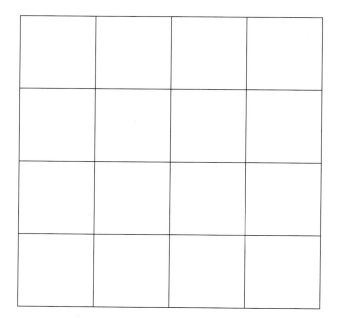

Choose 8 numbers to put in the empty box. Work out the differences between pairs of numbers. Write each difference in the grid.

Solve it!

Record your solutions here.

How did you solve it?

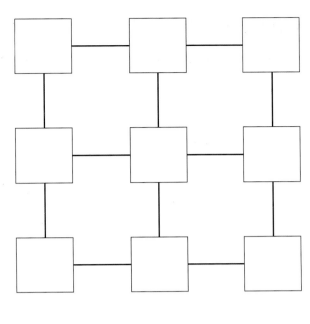

_____
_____
_____

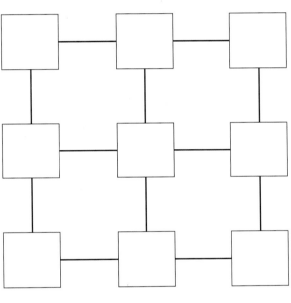

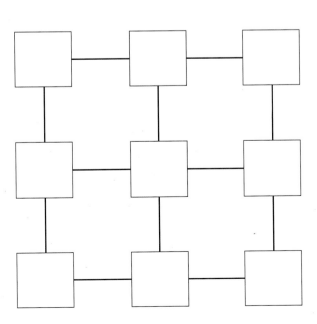

Equal totals

Make each row, column and diagonal have
the same total.
Find different ways.

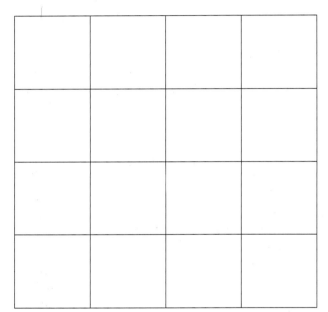

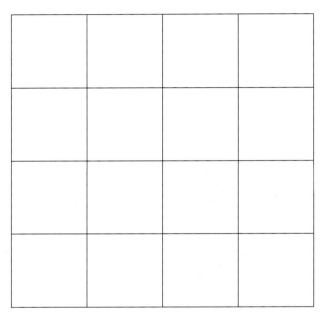

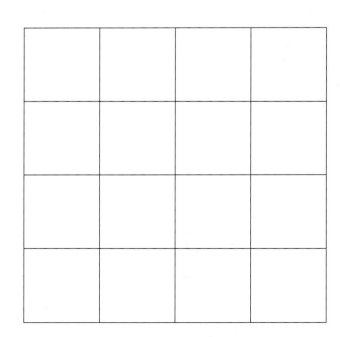

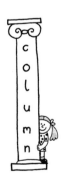

Leapfrog

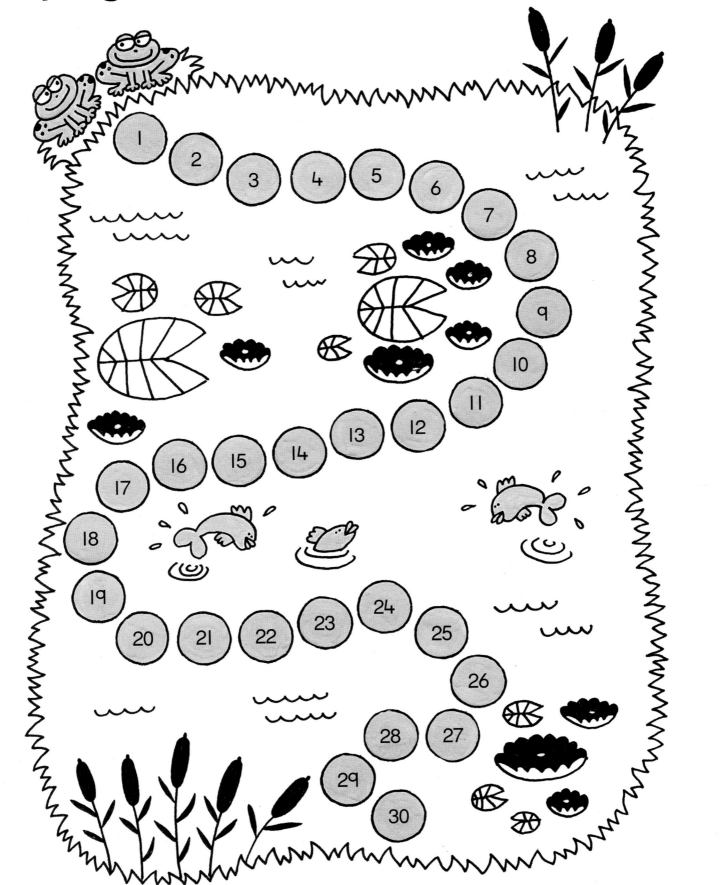

Shape tiles

2-D shapes

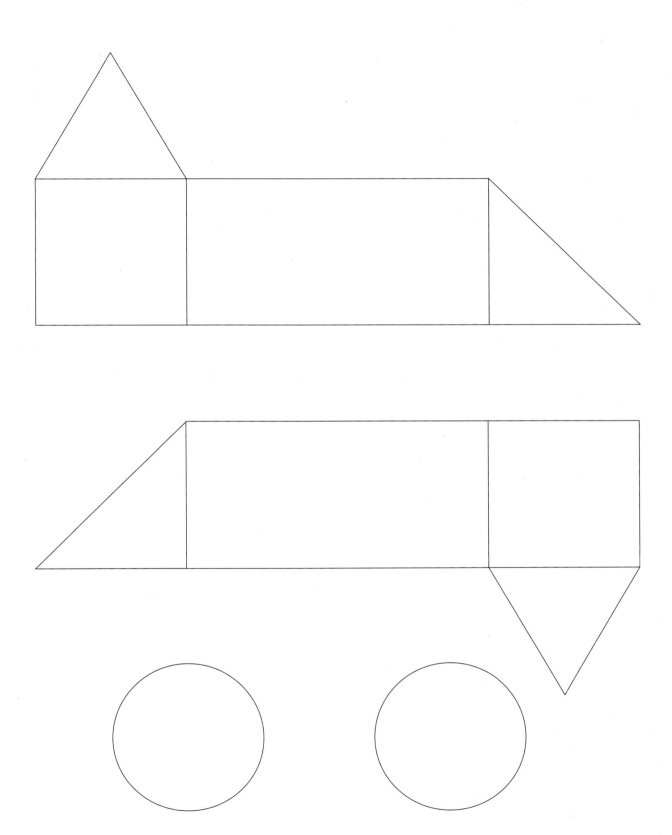

Shape pairs

Cut out the shapes. Fit them in pairs onto the shape on Textbook page 33.

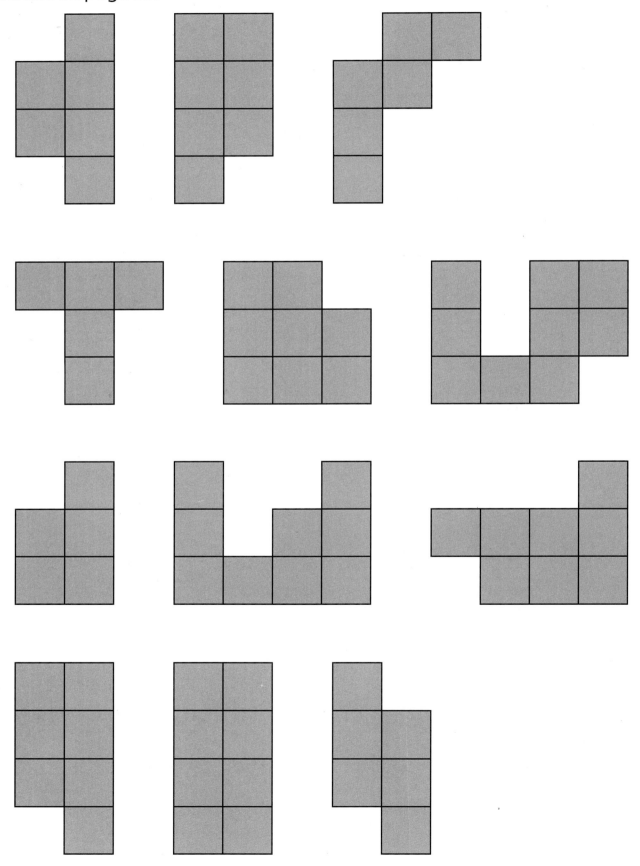

Clock faces

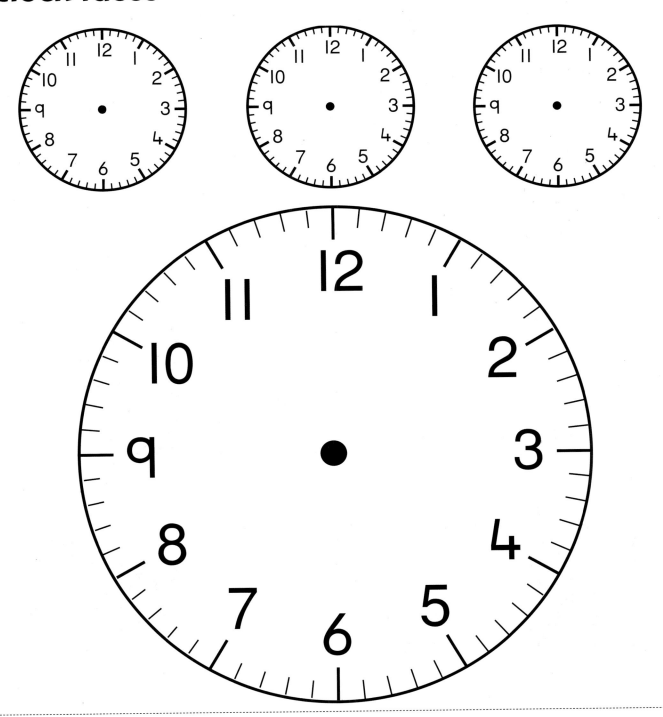

Cut out the hands.
Attach the hands to the large clock with a paper fastener.

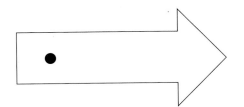 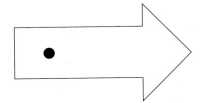

Name

Date

How old is Granny?

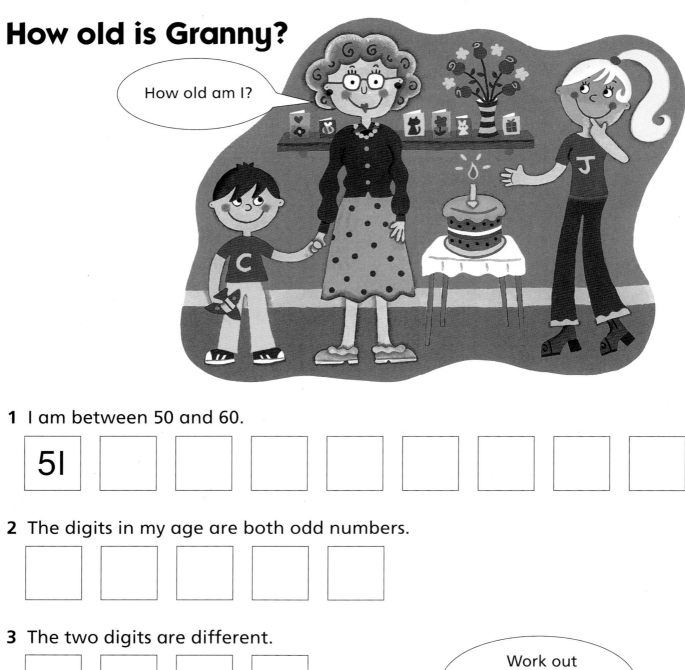

1 I am between 50 and 60.

5l								

2 The digits in my age are both odd numbers.

3 The two digits are different.

4 The difference between the two digits is 2.

Work out which numbers fit each clue.

5 The sum of the 2 digits is 12.

Granny is [ ] years old.